BE YOU

BE YOU

The Science of Becoming
the Self You Were Born to Be

Senka Holzer, PhD

NEW YORK

LONDON • NASHVILLE • MELBOURNE • VANCOUVER

BE YOU
The Science of Becoming the Self You Were Born to Be

Published in New York, New York, by Morgan James Publishing. Morgan James is a trademark of Morgan James, LLC. www.MorganJamesPublishing.com

At times, I tell stories to drive home my point. While the stories are true, I changed the names and identifying characteristics of some nice people to maintain their privacy—except for my husband and close friends. They don't care.

While the author has made every effort to provide accurate Internet addresses at the time of publication, neither the publisher nor the author assumes any responsibility for errors, or changes that occur after the publication.

Morgan James BOGO™

A **FREE** ebook edition is available for you or a friend with the purchase of this print book.

CLEARLY SIGN YOUR NAME ABOVE

Instructions to claim your free ebook edition:
1. Visit MorganJamesBOGO.com
2. Sign your name CLEARLY in the space above
3. Complete the form and submit a photo of this entire page
4. You or your friend can download the ebook to your preferred device

ISBN 978-1-63195-607-2 paperback
ISBN 978-1-63195-608-9 ebook
Library of Congress Control Number:
2021906834

Cover Design by:
Rachel Lopez
www.r2cdesign.com

Illustrations:
Tomislav Zlatic

Morgan James PUBLISHING Builds with... **Habitat for Humanity® Peninsula and Greater Williamsburg**

Morgan James is a proud partner of Habitat for Humanity Peninsula and Greater Williamsburg. Partners in building since 2006.

Get involved today! Visit
MorganJamesPublishing.com/giving-back

For Michi, David, and Jana.
To have a tool against me if I ever
start interfering with their core values.

Contents

Preface
(Please Don't Skip Me)

I grew up in a part of former Yugoslavia, a country now called Serbia. If the first thing that comes to your mind is war, I'm not surprised. The 1990s were a dark time in our history. Escalating tensions eventually led to civil wars (the plural is appropriate since there have been three). From today's perspective, those times were downright crazy. Money and food were scare. Toys? Non-existent.

It may be hard to imagine how kids like me could thrive under such circumstances, but there was freedom in having very little. Between the bombings and one of the largest inflations the world has ever seen, turning hard-earned money worthless overnight, being vulnerable was *normal*. This meant no one was worried about maintaining an "image." No one was "keeping up with the Joneses," and no one teased us for our worn-out shoes or not wearing the latest styles. And so the war gave me the rare opportunity to grow up with a sense of authenticity.

It wasn't until I was a young adult that I realized my experience of the world was unusual. During my time as an international research fellow at the University of California, Davis, I took a class called *Personal Foundation*. In that class, we studied (amongst other things) the concept of vulnerability—the idea that openly showing emotions is okay. During our discussion, my classmates erupted into tears around me as they admitted to powerful feelings, which they had been reluctant to demonstrate so openly. Yet, I sat there dry-eyed. I felt like an alien.

It took me days to understand my classmates' tears. I had always thought of vulnerability as a physical state of being, not the ability to open up emotionally. And I just *didn't get* why the idea of expressing emotions should be so complicated for people. Growing up in a war zone, my childhood friends and I didn't hold back when it came to saying we were scared, hurt, poor, or broken. *Everyone* around us was feeling that way—there was no point in pretending. So, it came as a surprise to me when I realized my classmates shared a real struggle when it came to being emotionally vulnerable.

On the one hand, my classmates couldn't admit to feeling unhappy, sad, or afraid because they didn't want to be seen as "weak;" on the other hand, they also felt the need to contain or minimize their joy and accomplishments. My friend Jessica once confessed to me that she waited three months before sharing the news of her engagement because she worried her single friends might think she was "showing-off." *Wow,* I thought, what must it be like to have second (and third and fourth) thoughts about saying, "I just got engaged, I'm so happy!"

I couldn't stop thinking about how much mental energy it must take to maintain a veneer of "toughness," "strength," and "modesty." I started asking myself questions: *What is this force that compels people to keep their emotions bottled up and guard their true selves? What is the motivation behind pretending to be happier/healthier/more secure than you are or dampening contentment and joy by guilt?* And the most important ones: *What else gets hidden when we hide our true emotions? What "big" choices are we making without input from our authentic selves?* The idea of this invisible force, lurking inside and preventing people from being exactly who they are, scared me more than the wars I saw growing up.

The more research I did, the more convinced I was that somewhere, somehow, we had gotten off track. We've been so busy living up to other's expectations that not being our authentic selves has become the *new normal.*

Vulnerability, I figured, was one stop along the way to authenticity (but definitely not the only one). I wondered what else—besides a willingness to be honest about our feelings—do we need to freely focus on the unique and innate talents, ideals, and passions we are born with? Then and there, in that classroom in Davis, California, I decided I want to use everything I learned in my scientific career to try and figure out why so many people struggle to be their beautiful, messy, authentic selves.

Over the last decade, and through many inspiring collaborations, I've used my free time to passionately develop science-based solutions that can coach people into *being* themselves. In this book, I'll share some of my biggest discoveries and show you how to translate the "big" ideas into tools for confronting and conquering your fear of being *you*.

THE WAR WITHIN

While you might not have experienced the chaos of a political war, the truth is, most of us are waging a war within ourselves, and we don't even know it. Sometimes, we let our default mode take over, putting out the fires one by one (what my friend calls, "the closest alligator to the boat"). But in moments of quiet transparency with ourselves, we recognize that something's not working. In fact, you've probably considered how, when, and what to change—but nothing's worked.

Even if you've identified the likely "change button" to press, the conversation with yourself probably went like this:

Well, Self, here's the thing . . .

I can't just leave my life/career/accomplishments/pursuits, etc., even though I don't feel very passionate about it.

OR

I'm overwhelmed by the thought of change, let alone the action it requires. I don't have time or energy for changing my life (now).

OR

By everyone's standards, I've got it made. What in the world is wrong with me that I still secretly long for XYZ?

I have firsthand experience with these sorts of conversation, and I *get* the challenge. But guess what? An extended failure to actively navigate the direction of our lives is not the answer. While I work primarily in the "molecular world," studying the diseases of the heart, I'm convinced that having a "healthy heart" means transferring our energy away from things that don't make us feel authentic, and, in some cases, do the exact opposite.

MY VISION

I know that with these new, intuitive, scientifically and empirically proven-to-work concepts you can gradually move away from looking *outside* and more toward looking *inside*. My vision is that, together, we can create the values matrix that celebrates *being you*—the self you were always meant to be, that curious, authentic, intrinsically driven, playful self, in harmony with others and the world you're living in.

Race For More

I have two pieces of news for you, one good and one bad. Which one do you want to hear first?

The bad one, of course.

Well, here it is: Something went terribly wrong in our modern world.

When we take the long view of humanity, we find so much to admire. We've made some formidable discoveries that are here to stay. Many diseases we once succumbed to can now be cured. The Internet has transformed how we gather and share information. We've created thousands and thousands of innovations, which even one hundred years ago would have been unthinkable. You'd expect we'd be feeling good about ourselves and our progress—that'd we'd be enjoying the comfortable lifestyle *we* created. You'd expect that we would be . . .

Fulfilled. At peace. Less afraid. Grateful.

But are we actually *more* fulfilled or at peace in modern times?

The simple answer is NO.

As humans, we've created a world that runs on keeping us in a state of constant questing, the phenomenon I call the "race for more." Ever since we evolved from hunter-gatherers into organized, agrarian societies, and as farming gave way to industrialization, social, political, and economic forces combined to infuse "get more for less" principles into all aspects of our lives. Economists tell us supply and demand drive innovation; politicians all over the globe prioritize improving economic growth; and social forces keep us pinning images of the newer "this" and improved "that" on our Pinterest boards.

This is especially true in the United States, where a whopping 68 percent of the GDP is based on personal consumption.[1] This *per se* is not the main problem, at least according to a dreamer and forever optimist like me. The real problem is that to maximize consumption, markets and the advertising industry opted for the fastest—but not the most beneficial and healthy way—to increase the money flow. That translated into generating a never-ending stream of "needs" based on fear, exploiting the weakest side of human nature[2]: *Oh my goodness, I have a wrinkle, I need that serum NOW!* Because of the billions of big and small fears like this, our economy is growing, but our focus is shifting more and more from thriving emotionally to thriving financially. We started believing that having, being, and reaching "more" is a (quick) fix to everything. But . . .

It's not working.

Infused with fears of "not having enough" and unhappy with our non-upgraded lives, we are "racing for more" on two levels: On the one hand, we're racing against *ourselves* trying to achieve "more," and on the other, we're racing against *others*, trying to document that our "more" is more than that of our peers'. In this race, many of us feel stuck in places that kill our creativity. We often feel overwhelmed and alone in our stories of giving it all. Sometimes, we even feel downright miserable, despite the fancy dishwasher and the giant TV. In the long run, this race leaves us living lives of constant unfulfillment, which creates wear and tear on our minds, bodies, and spirits and that worsens over time. (Anyone heard of burnout?)

RACING AGAINST OURSELVES: TEACHER OF THE YEAR

Nina is a single-mom who works full-time as a teacher. This wasn't the life she planned for, but she works hard so that her kids won't want for anything.

---

1   US Bureau of Economic Analysis, Shares of gross domestic product: Personal consumption expenditures [DPCERE1Q156NBEA], retrieved from FRED, Federal Reserve Bank of St. Louis; https://fred.stlouisfed.org/series/DPCERE1Q156NBEA, accessed February 10, 2021.

2   As a life scientist, I don't dare argue what would be a better option than a fear- and competition-based economic growth (unless it's past midnight at a social gathering, when I would mention soul-enhancing growth-based economy over a glass of dry Merlot).

She's up before 6:00 a.m. every day to style her hair, do her makeup, and choose the right outfit, even as she also gets the kids up and dressed—the importance of "looking appropriate" is surely something her mother had always impressed upon her. Many days, there isn't time for breakfast (well, priorities), and she and the kids grab sugary donuts on the way to school. In her classroom by 7:30 a.m., Nina's days are full. After teaching, she spends her afternoons in faculty meetings, working on new curriculum to impress the principal, lavishly decorating and cleaning her classroom (she's gunning for Teacher of the Year), and attending volunteer PTA meetings. These things are necessary, she thinks, if she's to get tenure and obtain job security, even if she is late for the Little League game or to pick up from Drama Club.

It's often past 7:00 p.m. when she finally leaves her classroom, rushing to finish errands or drop off meals for the elderly members of her church. Nina comes home exhausted, only to find dirty dishes in the sink. She snaps at her kids before falling into bed. Over time, her kids grow resentful and distant. So, Nina works harder to buy them tickets to Disneyland and new clothes—anything to make them happier. Sometimes, Nina cries herself to sleep at night. She's trying *so hard* to be the perfect parent, the perfect teacher, the perfect Christian, and the perfect member of the community. Why doesn't she feel more satisfied and fulfilled? Why doesn't anyone (including her kids) appreciate her effort?

Nina's story isn't a made-up example. She's the real-life mother of my friend, and her story isn't unique. We live in a world where it's common for one person to do the work formerly accomplished by two. At the end of the day, we have little energy left for the people and activities we love most. We find ourselves tired and unfocused, TV becomes a comfortable companion, and commercials never fail to remind us of the new video games, superfood supplements, and mega-volume mascara we "need."

And as if that isn't enough, there's "race for more" level two.

RACING AGAINST OTHERS: PERFECT AWARD CEREMONY

Ava is a CEO of a media empire (except she isn't, but stating her unique and high-ranking title would compromise her identity). She worked hard her whole life to tick all the success boxes you need to tick to earn social recognition and admiration.

At the time Ava was about to marry her first husband, approximately a year after their engagement, the two of them were having arguments on a daily basis. About what? Well, everything: where they wanted to live, how they would decorate the living room, where to travel for summer vacation, how often should they have sex. Basically, about everything you can think of. When her first husband left her four months into the marriage, she called me in despair every day for some weeks. During one of those conversations, she mentioned that her ex had asked her to postpone the wedding and rethink their decision to marry.

"And what did you tell him?" I asked curiously.

"That it's out of the question, of course. We already invited all those people, including the biggest media moguls in this country, so there's absolutely no way we could cancel the wedding," she replied in a single breath.

On the evening before the award ceremony where she was honored as the most influential CEO in the region, Ava had a terrible argument with Husband Number Two. By now, fights with her husband(s) were nothing new. But when he told her that he was not going to join the ceremony the next day, she was horrified. She immediately called me and cried, "What will people think when he's not there tomorrow? Everyone will *know* we had an argument." I knew that whatever I said wouldn't change the scenario for tomorrow or any day in Ava's future—I'd been arguing with her without success for years. Just as she pushed her first husband into their wedding, she finally pushed the next one into attending the award ceremony. Thank goodness because how else would she post the most spectacular and most glamorous photos of the happiest power-couple on earth on every existing social media platform? #powerwoman #CEOoftheyear #powercouple #family

You may laugh at Ava's story or think she's crazy, but if you go deeper, you'll realize that she's surely not the only one who feels the pressure to show the world she's winning the game of life. It won't take you too long to find examples of how you decorate events from your own life to release them to the public in the form of stories, comments, photos, blogs, or videos.

In our race to afford it all and broadcast that we achieved "more" than the others, we silently agree to trade a big chunk of our time and energy for money. We enroll in self-promotion and competition. In turn, we become more and more tied to our jobs (no matter how stressful or draining they are), and we accept the myth that living on the edge of burnout is a legitimate route to success and ultimate fulfillment.

What "More" Do You Want More of?

Don't worry, I haven't forgot the good news.

The good news is that we can rewrite problematic pages of our history and correct wrongly calculated formulas by increasing our awareness and understanding the limitations in our current paths. To do so, we must understand that yes, indeed, we can have more—but the fear-motivated "more" that our society promotes comes at a price. I hope this book will encourage you to ask yourself: Is this "more" really the best kind of "more" for me?

In this book, you'll have the opportunity to learn how, fueled by fear, we became "programmed" to detach from our own passions, disconnect from others, and regard ourselves as separate from nature, while enthusiastically striving for society's definition of "more." You'll then learn how, in order to connect authentically with ourselves and others, we must slow down the constant hustle. Only in moments of stillness can we pay attention to the things that are draining our energy; only then can we reprogram our behaviors, drop the "race for more," and make space for kindness, compassion, curiosity, and growth—the essence of a more joyful living.

How? I knew you'd ask. Understanding your psychological needs and values is a surefire way to help you feel good about yourself and every decision you make, from which t-shirt to buy, where you want to live and which career you want to pursue to what to text back to your partner or how to behave in times of large-scale crisis (because I intensively worked on this book in 2020, I can't stop thinking of toilet paper). When you understand what *being you* is really about, you'll know which kind of "more" will help you achieve your full potential and unleash the wild creativity lying within you.

THE "BIG" IDEAS—A SNEAK PREVIEW

In addition, we'll explore how you're ultimately guided by the three concepts that form the foundation in this book:

1. Core versus Acquired Values
2. The Rhetoric-Reality Gap
3. The Expectation-Reality Gap

My research as a scientist and professional experience as a coach have proven, over and over, that these three concepts are at the heart of our dissatisfaction—as individuals and as a society.

1. CORE VERSUS ACQUIRED VALUES

We make all of our choices based on our values, consciously or unconsciously. Everything from picking a career path to deciding which toothpaste to buy is an expression of our values.

Values are our perception of what matters most in life—something we feel driven to attain. One of the most important discoveries from my scientific work is that we have not one, but two sets of values. That's right, TWO.

Core Values:

We are born with our core values. They are the things that give us pure joy, the things that matter more than anything else. When we align our lives with our core values, we're at our best.

Too theoretical? Imagine a little boy stealing money from his parents to buy bird food. Watching the flow of tiny seeds pouring into the carefully crafted birdhouse makes his heart sing. He quickly loses sense of time and forgets about the punishment waiting for him when he returns home. He is purely in the moment.

This awesome little boy is now my husband. And he keeps feeding birds with the same passion and joy thirty years later (only now he doesn't have to steal money to do it because, ahem, I'm the value expert). You won't be surprised to hear that two of his top core values are *appreciating nature* and *helping others*.

Acquired Values:

We all acquire values from many outside sources: family, friends, the (social) media, our generation, and our culture. The world(s) around us give us models to follow. This is absolutely normal. It's how we make it through childhood and ultimately become good citizens.

To understand this second set of values, consider a young woman (a.k.a. my bestie) who is about to enroll in college. She only has a slight awareness of what truly makes her tick (traveling, coffee, and her dog), yet she is persistently told that her life, status, and fulfillment, all depend on choosing the right profession. Programmed to believe the right profession is stable, challenging—so you have to work really hard—and high paying, she enrolled in technical engineering. Because she made choices rooted in values she acquired from her parents (*status, hard-work,* and *wealth*), she struggled to pay attention and had to force herself to complete each assignment. It took her eleven years to earn a degree.

We need to take the time to distinguish between our core and acquired values because even "big things"—the corner office, the nice house, or a technical engineer title—rooted in our acquired values won't bring us the same genuine fulfillment as "feeding the birds." When acquired values overshadow our core values, we enter the rat race—a self-defeating, pointless, but hard-to-break pursuit.

Understanding that we have those two different sets of values gives us the tools to align our choices, big and small, with what matters most to us, jettisoning the dead weight of external "shoulds." And that is all we need to be courageously authentic.

2. THE RHETORIC-REALITY GAP

Sometimes what we *say* is most important to us is not the same as what we actually *do.* For example, a parent may believe whole-heartedly that they are greatly committed to their kids—that nurturing the relationship with their kids is their top priority. Yet, when they read an article saying that an average working parent spends only seven minutes of actual conversation a day with their kids, and subsequently analyze their typical day, they may be astounded to see that their schedule tells a similar story.

We experience a gap—a mismatch—between our rhetoric and our reality when we respond to situations automatically, without making conscious choices. Because our acquired values cruise along with a strong tailwind of repetitive "shoulds," they can quickly push us to react to what seems most urgent, acceptable, or even inevitable. *I should work harder, I should keep my house cleaner. I should exercise every day. I shouldn't ask for help.* We unconsciously follow what was modeled for us and move away from what really matters to us, creating the Rhetoric-Reality Gap.

3. THE EXPECTATION-REALITY GAP

We adopt many acquired values based on persistent external voices, some loud and others subtle, which urge us to behave in specific ways. To make their case convincing, external sources always promise a reward. Have you ever made a choice because you expected a specific, positive outcome? Common examples of expectations that can create a gap between expectations and reality include:

> *A well-paying job will make me happy.*
> *Earning straight As will secure me a rewarding career.*
> *Climbing the corporate hierarchy will increase my self-confidence.*
> *Being fit/thin will attract the best partner.*
> *Staying strong at any cost will earn me a good reputation.*

We inherit these reward-driven models from our elders, peers, and social environments. We see what's worked for others and work hard to follow in their footsteps, creating personal goals based on values acquired from outside. As high-achieving people, we often meet—or exceed—our goals. We got the promotion, billed the most hours, graduated in the top 1 percent, found a good partner and had two kids, built an impressive financial portfolio, all while maintaining six-pack abs. We've lived up to our end of the bargain, right? We initially experience a spike of good feeling, but it quickly fades away, and we're left feeling dissatisfied and wanting more. We wait for the promised reward . . . and wait . . . and wait.

The pleasure we expected as a result of all of our achievements still feels elusive. We feel unhappy, dissatisfied, depressed, and, as a result, we question all of our choices. We question ourselves. We learn the hard way that meeting certain goals rarely produces the sustained, intense fulfillment we expect. I call this effect "The Expectation-Reality Gap."

My research proves one particularly important point: We're more likely to experience an Expectation-Reality Gap if the goal we're chasing is driven by an acquired value rather than a core value. In contrast, there is a strong correlation between achieving a goal based on a core value and lasting happiness.

Now, let's dive into the details.

I.

The Building Blocks
Of Being You

Chapter 1

Your Psychological Needs

If you missed out on the infamous college course that everyone loves to hate, never fear! In this chapter, I'll share a few groundbreaking theories in modern psychology. The ideas gathered here represent some of the most important scientific discoveries in humanity's quest to understand ourselves. While you won't walk away with a degree, or even a minor you can use to torment your family members at holiday dinners, my hope is that you will have a better understanding of your own psychological needs and how to ask that those needs be met in healthy ways. I am going to guide you on a journey to the center of you, helped along the way by science and philosophy.

WELCOME TO PSYCH 101

Modern science is a marvel. Every day, we learn more about our universe, our planet, and ourselves. Exciting developments in neuroscience are making it possible to understand human nature in ways we've never seen before. As a result, we are coming closer and closer to answering some of humanity's "Big Existential Questions." We are learning how to tune in to our own bodies and identify what makes us happy and healthy (a.k.a. our ultimate fulfillment). But science alone isn't enough to bring us fully into the lives we were meant to live. We also need a willingness to look inside ourselves.

THE PURSUIT OF HAPPINESS

What do we need to be happy?

Ah, the age-old question. Across our planet's many cultures, people have been asking and answering this question for a long time. Aristotle, for example, believed that wellbeing and fulfillment came from doing the things that reflect our true calling in life—what we might also call our "nature." Not buying it? You aren't the only one.

Sigmund Freud (we couldn't have Psych 101 without him, could we?), the father of psychoanalysis, had a *somewhat* opposite view of human nature. For Freud, human beings are basically irrational. We are forever driven by irrational, practically uncontrollable, *id* instincts—sex and aggression—which lie outside the sphere of the conscious and are "the ultimate cause of all activity."[3] Or, as psychologist Stephen Joseph explained in plain English, Freud seemed to be saying that we humans would be "lustful, murderous savages if we followed our natural instincts, and it was only through civilization that we learned to check our destructive nature."[4,5] These days, we tend to take a dim view of Freud's analysis of human nature, but the credit goes to Freud for being the first to recognize that our intention to satisfy our desires, wants, and needs drives our behavior, and failure to satisfy these needs and wants results in a state of anxiety or tension (and also that joke about a cigar).

As Freudian thinking gave way to modern humanistic psychology (in 1950s and '60s), psychologists Carl Rogers and Abraham Maslow started revisiting Aristotle. Their subsequent theories were considered controversial because they contrasted sharply with the widely accepted school of Behaviorism (Watson 1925). Behaviorism argues that all human behaviors are acquired through conditioning, and conditioning crept into every pore of Western culture, from childrearing and education to policies that intended to regulate and control people. However,

---

3   Ziegler, Daniel J., Freud, Rogers, and Ellis: "A Comparative Theoretical Analysis." *Journal of Rational-Emotive and Cognitive-Behavior Therapy*, 2002.

4   Joseph, Stephen, PhD. "Authentic: How To Be Yourself and Why It Matters." *Piatkus*, 2017.

5   Joseph, Stephen, PhD. "Are Authentic People More Self-Interested." *Psychology Today*. 24 July 2016, Accessed 10 Feb 2021, https://www.psychologytoday.com/us/blog/what-doesnt-kill-us/201607/are-authentic-people-more-self-interested, included with permission from the author.

according to Rogers and Maslow, we don't need social institutions to shape us into constructive members of society. We need social structures that help us identify and put into practice our innate skills and potentials in ways that contribute positively to our wellbeing and the wellbeing of those around us.[6]

Midterm Exam!

If you've been paying good attention, you should be able to answer the following question:

What has been the central debate in modern psychology?

Your brilliant minds got it right. The central debate in modern psychology has been: *Should our fundamental human nature be controlled or liberated by society?* Today, psychologists tend to agree on the latter.

Beyond the Carrot and the Stick: Modern Psychological Theory Turns Inward

In the 1970s, Dr. Richard Ryan and Dr. Edward Deci began collaborating at the University of Rochester to better understand our internal motivation. Together, they developed the Self-Determination Theory, a far-reaching psychological theory that examines what drives us at our deepest levels.[7] Rooted in the belief that we should aim to liberate human nature, they demonstrated the limits of punishments and rewards as successful motivators. In doing so, Ryan and Deci unseated the dominant Behaviorist view that we need to be tightly regulated, monitored, and shaped into being ideal members of society.

Specifically, Deci and Ryan discovered that intrinsic motivations are more powerful than the external motivators of rewards and punishments. Furthermore, they identified three basic psychological needs, which all humans share: **autonomy, competence,** and **relatedness**. Regardless of our stage of human development, our culture, or our environmental circumstances, we *all* share these same three needs. When these needs are met, we thrive. When they

---

6   Joseph, Stephen, PhD. *Authentic: How to Be Yourself and Why It Matters.* Piatkus, 2017.

7   Richard M. Ryan, & Edward L. Deci. Self-determination theory: Basic psychological needs in motivation, development, and wellness. *Guilford Press,* 2017

are in short supply, we struggle and are motivated to find ways to meet them. This may seem obvious to us, but . . .

In the world of psychology, this was BIG.

Researchers have cited Ryan and Deci's foundational paper over 40,000 times (there's an average of four citations per paper), making it the Gangnam Style of motivational psychology.[8] Self-Determination Theory has inspired thousands of studies backing the theory while hundreds of researchers use it as the foundation of their work.

NEEDS VERSUS WANTS

Deci and Ryan defined a "need" as something that negatively affects our wellbeing when we are deprived of it. Likewise, a satisfied need positively impacts our wellbeing. We may "want" something and think we desperately need it to be happy, but that desire may not help us thrive—and may even be detrimental.

WANT

NEED

MOST OF US DON'T NEED A MEME TO
UNDERSTAND THE DIFFERENCE BETWEEN A
NEED AND A WANT. BUT WHO WOULDN'T
WANT ONE?

---

8   https://livingmeanings.com/three-needs-you-need-to-fulfill-for-well-being/ (updated from Google Scholar)

This cheeky meme captures the essence of a need—*I might want more ice cream, but another carton of butter pecan caramel probably won't enhance my health and wellness*. A downer, I know.

No matter how much we may resist separating a need from a want or how dismissive we may be about a particular need, the effects of need deprivation are real, whether we believe them to be important or not. As Ryan and Deci put it: "[. . .] whether or not one subjectively appreciates vitamin C, its extended deprivation *will* lead to scurvy."[9]

Let's take a closer look at each of these three needs: autonomy, competency, and relatedness. Relatedness means connecting with other people and not being a loner. To simplify, I'll use the word "connection" instead.

"My Way"[10]

What does it mean to live with **autonomy**? It has a lot in common with how I define authenticity. Living autonomously means being true to yourself, no matter what others say you *should* do or think. Simply put, autonomy is our need to feel that we're in charge of our own life and choices.

It sounds obvious. You may be thinking, *Of course I am in charge of my life and my choices—why wouldn't I be?* And yet, as I think you will come to understand as you read this book, autonomy may be something essential that we all need, but not all of us are actually living our lives autonomously.

An astonishing number of people in the Western world express regret over not living an autonomous life when on their deathbeds. Bonnie Ware, a palliative-care nurse, heard so many of these confessions from her dying patients that she was inspired to write an article on deathbed reflections for the *Huffington Post* (which she later turned into a best-selling book[11]). She writes of the brutal clarity people gain toward the end of their lives—a clarity that contains much wisdom for the living.

---

9   Ryan, Richard M. and Edward L. Deci. "Self-Determination Theory: Basic Psychological Needs in Motivation, Development, and Wellness." *Guilford Press*, 2017.
10   A nod to . . . Frank Sinatra. "My Way." *My Way*. Sonny Burke, 1969.
11   Ware, Bronnie. *The Top Five Regrets of the Dying: A Life Transformed by the Dearly Departing.* San Diego: Hay House Inc., 2012, reprint.

Over time, Ware noticed a pattern in the final regrets of her patients. One regret, in particular, stood out as the most commonly repeated by the dying: *I wish I'd had the courage to live a life true to myself, not the life others expected of me.*

Ouch. Ware's observations, backed by studies about regret, reveal that when people look back on their lives as they near death, they aren't grateful for following the rules, playing it safe, or following the advice of others. No. They regret living the life others expected of them. They regret not living a life aligned with their authentic selves. They regret their unfulfilled dreams.

We, the living, have an incredible opportunity to learn from these observations. We can make choices that are aligned with who we are—choices that allow us to be authentic and autonomous. It's not easy to let go of the expectations of others, and much of this book is devoted to helping you make the courageous choices that serve your unique purpose in life. As you read the following chapter, I'll be asking you frequently to think about your ideal life. But, just for a moment, can you imagine your ideal death? Will you die mourning the roads not taken and wondering what would or could have been? Or will you die peacefully, even happily? Perhaps you'll be humming along to the that final verse of Frank Sinatra's "My Way."

"HEIGH HO, HEIGH HO (IT'S OFF TO WORK WE GO)"[12]

Consider a moment in your life when you experienced a feeling of **competence**. What were you doing? Was it working in a certain job? Solving a problem or answering a tough question? Winning an award or special recognition? Maybe it was seeing something you had envisioned take shape just as you had imagined it would. How did you feel in that moment?

We feel competent when the choices we've made and the effort we've put into something result in a positive outcome. We feel competent when we feel we've made a contribution to our tribe for the greater good.

One way researchers have measured the impact of competency has been through comparing the psychological health of unemployed and employed persons. Research shows that our wellbeing is negatively affected when we don't

---

12   A nod to Frank Churchill's (lyrics written by Larry Morey), "Heigh Ho, Heigh Ho (It's Off to Work We Go)" from Disney's *Snow White*, 1937.

have a job.[13] Sure, when we're out of work, many of us worry about how to make ends meet without the security of a regular paycheck. But the unhappiness goes even deeper, studies show. Our salary, the financial reward for our efforts, is important, but it's just one piece of our wellbeing. Having a job also provides us with purpose, creativity, and engagement. We feel competent when our efforts are valued.

Let's take Sweden as an example. The Scandinavian nation is known for strong social systems that support citizens when they are in need. In Sweden, losing a job doesn't automatically mean financial insecurity. The state supports workers until they are back on their feet. Free of worry over how to pay bills and put food on the table, you'd think that unemployed Swedes would be less stressed and happier than their unemployed American counterparts. That's because we may be thinking of employment as solely a means to a financial ends. In fact, a study of recently unemployed persons in Sweden found that out-of-workers experienced a loss of dignity as human beings, even though their financial security was still intact, thanks to the country's policies. Losing a job means much more than losing income, the participants in the study shared. When they stopped contributing, they suffered. As their basic need for competence went unmet, insecurity and worry battered their self-esteem, and they eventually isolated themselves from their friends and family.

We are miraculously resilient, and it's common for us to adapt to life events. Evidence suggests that when we have an adverse experience, such as a divorce, severe physical injuries, or the loss of a house to a natural disaster, our wellbeing initially decreases, but over time, we become used to the new experience or environment. Our level of wellbeing returns to the previous level.

This is NOT true, however, for unemployment. We do not adapt when we don't have jobs— most likely because having a job is a primary way for us to feel competent. Without our basic need of competence met, we may feel directionless and worthless.

We all have bad days at work; we may even hate our jobs or our bosses at times. And while we may not always sing our way through our morning

---

13   Lucas, Richard E., Clark Andrew E., et al. "Unemployment Alters the Set Point For Life Satisfaction." *Psychology Science*, 2004.

commute like Snow White's Seven Dwarfs (or the character, Michael Bolton, from the opening scene of *Office Space*), our wellbeing and self-worth depend on feeling competent.

"I Wanna' Dance With Somebody (Who Loves Me)"[14]

As Her Royal Divaness Whitney Houston reminds us: We all need to feel connected to each other and feel that we belong. We need champions and teammates, those people we can call in the middle of the night, the ones who will never hesitate to make a last-minute airport run or show up on moving day without complaint. **Connection** is our third and final basic human need.

For most of our human history, while we lived in tribes, disconnecting from our people knocked out our chances of survival (recall the wise words of *Game of Throne*'s Ned Stark about what happens to the lone wolfs?[15]). Meanwhile, those who stuck together enjoyed more safety, more mating, and more resources. As we transitioned into a modern society, we learned belonging is not only essential for our survival, but it's one of our deepest human desires.

Many studies highlight the importance of connection, but one in particular stands out. For over seventy-five years, researchers at Harvard tracked the lives of over 700 men as part of The Harvard Study of Adult Development.[16] The study, designed to help researchers identify what makes us happy and healthy, is the longest investigation of adult life completed to date and consisted of two groups of men: sophomores at Harvard College and boys from Boston's poorest neighborhoods.

Every year since 1938, researchers visited the men in their living rooms, asking them extensive questions about their work, home life, and health. They also acquired their medical records, drew blood, and scanned their brains. When the participants began having children, they talked to the kids as well. They videotaped the men talking with their wives about their successes and failures, their moments of joy and despair.

---

14 Houston, Whitney. "I Wanna' Dance With Somebody (Who Loves Me)." *Whitney.* Hal Leonard Publishing Corp., 1987.

15 Martin, George R.R. *A Song of Ice and Fire (Book One).* New York: Bantam, 2002, reprint.

16 "The Study of Adult Development," Division of Psychiatry, Brigham and Women's Hospital, Boston, MA, 2014.

The study wrapped up in 2013. As the Harvard experts sifted through and analyzed seventy-five years' worth of data, one factor appeared over and over as a significant contributor to the happiness of the men: relationships. Robert Waldinger, the study's director, explained in his TED talk, "The clearest message that we got from this seventy-five-year study is this: Good relationships keep us happier and healthier. Period."[17]

The study concluded that our social ties play a more important role than social class, IQ, or even genes, reinforcing the messages pop music has been sending us for years—meaningful relationships with others make us happy. It turns out that people who are more socially connected to family, friends, and their community are happier and physically healthier.

Researchers were also able to conclude that people who experience more isolation are less happy and live shorter lives than people who are not lonely. Sadly, loneliness is at epidemic levels in America. Nearly half of Americans report feeling lonely, while more and more people report feeling left out, poorly understood, and lacking companionship.[18]

This leads us to the study's second big takeaway—quality over quantity. The study showed that we don't need lots of friends or a "successful" partnership to be happy. Indeed, many of us may have felt lonely in a partnership or damaged by family conflicts. What matters is the quality of our close relationships. One loyal friend contributes more to our wellbeing than dozens of matching-t-shirt-wearing relatives or hundreds of followers on social media.

THE HARVARD STUDY OF ADULT DEVELOPMENT—A (SHORT) PLAYLIST

"The Power of Love," Huey Lewis and the News

"A Little Help From My Friends," The Beatles

"Love Will Keep Us Together," Captain and Tennille

"Stand By Me," Ben E. King

---

17 Waldinger, Robert. 2015. "What Makes a Good Life? Lessons From the Longest Study On Happiness." Uploaded on November 15, 2015. YouTube video, 12:39 min. https://www.ted.com/talks/robert_waldinger_what_makes_a_good_life_lessons_from_the_longest_study_on_happiness/transcript.

18 Cigna's national survey exploring the impact of loneliness in the United States; 18 Dec 2018, https://www.cigna.com/newsroom/news-releases/2018/pdf/new-cigna-study-reveals-loneliness-at-epidemic-levels-in-america.pdf.

"Crazy Little Thing Called Love," Queen
"Lean on Me," Bill Wither
"Is This Love," Bob Marley and the Wailers
"We Found Love," Rihanna, feat. Calvin Harris
"You're the Inspiration," Chicago
"You Got A Friend in Me," Randy Newman
"My Love Don't Cost A Thing," Jennifer Lopez
"Time After Time," Cyndie Lauper
"I'll Be There," The Jackson Five
"Love Will Keep Us Alive," The Eagles
"We're Going To Be Friends," The White Stripes
"Wouldn't It Be Nice," Beach Boys
"Cheap Thrills," Sia
"Started From the Bottom," Drake

Homework: Add your favorite song to the playlist to celebrate your precious relationships!

OUR GREATEST SUPERPOWER: INTRINSIC MOTIVATION

When we satisfy our three basic needs, we unlock our greatest superpower—our intrinsic motivation (read this again). We're intrinsically motivated to do something when we engage in an activity for its own sake. It's the opposite of the extrinsic motivation—when we do something in order to earn a reward or avoid a punishment.

While both intrinsic and extrinsic motivation are important and can coexist, they can have different effects on our behaviors and how we pursue goals. When we are intrinsically motivated, we perform better, especially in the long term. We feel more passionately about our intrinsic motivators and are personally committed to acting on them. Intrinsic motivations help us through difficulties more successfully than extrinsic motivations, while also enhancing our creativity, innovation, and problem-solving potential.

So, when our motivation truly comes from within, we're more likely to experience joy, fulfillment and success. We can increase our chances of being intrinsically motivated when we feel self-directed, competent, and connected—when all of our three basic needs are being met.

CONTEMPORARY ACROBATS: JUGGLING OUR THREE NEEDS IN A FAST-PACED WORLD

Here's what's important to know about satisfying our three needs and unlocking our intrinsic motivation: we cannot psychologically thrive by satisfying one need alone. Just as humans can't live on water without food nor plants in soil without sunlight, we need *all three* of our basic needs met in order to thrive.

For example, when we have ample opportunities to experience competence but lack meaningful connections with others (or vice versa), our wellbeing suffers. Consider the taxing career paths that take us away from spending time with our significant others. Or the child of demanding and controlling parents who learns to relinquish autonomy to feel loved.[19]

Yet, for most of us, it's challenging to satisfy all of our needs simultaneously because we have only twenty-four hours a day. We often get off track when we think that only once we have professional or financial success can we dedicate our time to our needs, or when we believe we can satisfy all three needs during our limited free time. When that happens, we pretty much have no chance of making it work. If we're lucky, we might have a few hours a day of free time—not nearly enough to pursue projects that make us feel competent and autonomous while nourishing our meaningful relationships. We also risk burnout chasing prestigious jobs and titles. But if we find fulfillment in our work through projects and assignments that give us a sense of competence and autonomy, then a good portion of our free time will be reserved for nurturing close relationships, restoring the much-needed balance for us.

We can't keep a perfect balance between all three needs all of the time. When you get the promotion you've always dreamed about, you'll naturally press the gas pedal on your competence need. If you get married or become a parent, you'll drift toward connection (and forget your autonomy for a while in the case of latter). That's okay. What's important is to cultivate a general

---

19   Ryan, Richard M. Ryan and Edward L. Deci. *Self-Determination Theory: Basic Psychological Needs in Motivation, Development, and Wellness.*

mindfulness toward all three needs and a long-term plan for having all three needs met in the future.

Despite our innate yearning for autonomy, competence, and connection, many of us don't chart the courses of our lives by these three cardinal points. When we learn to take an active role in aligning our actions with the pursuit of our three basic needs, we can feel confident we're headed in the right direction.

Fair enough, you might be saying, but where do I begin? How do I break down these "big ideas" so that I can make noticeable changes in my daily life? After all, if it were so easy to find love, we'd have no Tinder, no *The Bachelor*, and artists and musicians would have a lot less material to work with. If competency could be easily attained, I'd never experience burnout and we'd have no need for "productivity courses," motivational TED talks, and annual reviews.

This is where my research comes in. I've discovered that we all have a unique "psychological DNA," a preset code for fulfilling our three basic needs. This code is actually made up of our core values. Our core values connect our basic needs with our behavior. When we can identify and understand our core values, we can support and balance our basic need for autonomy, competency, and connection. Our core values are the building blocks for genuine fulfillment. As you learn to recognize your intrinsic motivators, you're taking the first step in a transformative process that will take you from feeling hungry for meaning to finding purpose and ultimate fulfillment.

Chapter 2

Your Core Values

In an ideal world, we could read the previous chapter and say, *Great! Now that I know what I need in order to thrive, I'm going to make an action plan and adjust my actions and behaviors so they serve my three basic psychological needs.* The reality is way more complicated than that (in case you haven't noticed).

It's All Connected

Each of Self-Determination Theory's three basic psychological needs could be broken into smaller components—**core values**. Think of the need for *connection.* Values like *trust, loyalty, humor, optimism, respect, responsibility, caring, awareness,* or *discipline* are important aspects of many people's need for healthy connection with others. But the specific combination of values that fulfill our needs differs from person to person. While we all share the same three basic needs, your special matrix of values distinguishes you from me, your brother, a neighbor, or the person with your same name on the other side of the world. Your unique values are what makes you, you. Core values are a reflection of *what matters most to you,* and they tend to be fixed—that is, your core values don't change as you grow up or as your life circumstances change.

In his research on life values, Milton Rokeach, a Polish-American social psychologist (ranked as one of the 100 most eminent psychologists of the twentieth century) revealed another important piece of information we need to know to thrive: not only do our values fulfill our basic psychological needs, our values also drive our behavior.[20] Our behavior reflects how much we value something. For example, if you value *adventure*, then you likely won't travel to the same familiar city and stay in the same familiar hotel where the receptionist knows your extended family by name every summer. If you value *nature*, you'll enjoy time outdoors, and you'll recycle and reduce packaging. Our values matrix controls our functioning, connecting our basic needs with our behaviors.

Think about something you can do for hours without feeling tired. Whatever activity you're imagining is linked to one of your core values. Miguel loves to read fashion magazines and follows rising models on Instagram. In his spare time, he designs his own special "looks" and enjoys sharing them with friends. For Miguel, these activities reflect his core values of *appearance, creativity,* and *design/art.* Miguel feels intrinsically motivated to study the latest trends and try them out at home. The activities themselves are their own reward.

The same is true for all of us. We pursue our core values without the threat of punishment or the promise of a reward. When we are acting in alignment with a core value, we feel excited and motivated. Miguel's **behaviors** reflect his **core values** and the competency and authenticity he experiences while designing and sharing new styles satisfies his **basic psychological needs**.

THE TREE OF LIFE

The interplay between your psychological needs, your core values, and your behavior are what *being you* is all about. In a healthy person, all three components work to help us thrive. Imagine the apple tree to the right represents your life.

In order for the apple tree to thrive (and produce a lot of apples) it needs strong roots. Strong roots help grow a big treetop with an abundance of leaves. The leaves, in turn, are in charge of photosynthesis. Flashback to grade school science: photosynthesis is the chemical process plants use to turn light, carbon dioxide, and water into functional energy (sugars). The resulting sugars fuel the tree's growth cycle, including its root system and fruit.

Our needs, values, and behaviors are similarly linked. Our needs for autonomy, competence, and connection form our roots and solid foundation.

---

20   Rokeach, Milton. *Understanding Human Values.* Washington, D.C.: Free Press, 2000.

Like the trunk and branches of a tree, our values connect our needs to our behaviors, represented by the leaves.

When our basic needs are satisfied (strong roots), we have high levels of intrinsic motivation, so we engage in many actions (many leaves). Because these actions arise from our core values, they reinforce the satisfaction of our needs in return. The whole system runs in a positive loop, and we experience wellbeing; we bear fruit.

NEVER STOP NEVER STOPPING

Making positive life changes would be easier if our core values worked like our five senses. Imagine being able to pinpoint our values as easily as we see colors, feel the warmth of the sun, or smell the ocean breeze. *Check out the brilliant blue feathers on that bird . . . check out my loyalty value working . . .*

But most of us have a hazy and incomplete understanding of our core values. Some of us may have a general sense of what works for us—and what doesn't—but we haven't yet processed those insights through a core values matrix. For example, Maryam may know that waking up at 5:45 a.m. every day to do yoga boosts her productivity and makes her feel good, but she may not consciously link her behavior to *structure, productivity,* and *mindfulness*—her core values.

I remember when our professor asked us to list our core values in my *Personal Foundation* class. All of us (yes, me included) weren't sure. Although we were in the course because we were all fascinated with self-development, we found it difficult to describe what matters most to us. It came as a surprise. I had several degrees and a decade of work experiences, but I still struggled to comprehend and articulate my inner workings.

Today, I know one of my top core values is *motivation*. Motivating others to make positive changes gives me a sense of purpose, as well as inner peace and satisfaction. Although I was over thirty before I identified motivation as a core value, when I look back, I can see how motivation has always been important to me. I remember how I purposefully played with the kids who felt sad or excluded in kindergarten. On a field trip in elementary school, I volunteered to be roommates with a girl others avoided. As an adult, I make a conscious choice to spend my time and resources on the underdogs. If I see two restaurants next to each other, one filled with customers and the other empty, I choose the latter because I hope the workers will feel better and enjoy a flash of motivation. I often find myself giving impromptu pep talks and coaching sessions to strangers sitting next to me on planes. I can't help it; it's just who I am!

I wasn't guided in my behavior toward others by my parents, teachers, or other authority figures. I feel naturally driven to motivate others. My enjoyment comes from watching people's moods improve, not from a place of pity or compliment-seeking. My desire to light a spark of motivation comes from a place of joy inside me.

Who can relate? What things do you do without prompting or reminders? What are you doing when time seems to fly by? What can't you help but do or be? What makes you want to #neverstop?

INSIDE OUT: OUR "PSYCHOLOGICAL DNA"

While we live in the age of genetic testing, where anyone with $99 and a tube-full of saliva can have the mysteries of their genetics delivered to their inbox, how much do you really remember about DNA, genes, and genetics? If you're not a science nerd like me, you probably need a brief review.

Our physical bodies, including all of the visible traits like hair, eye and skin color, height, and body shape and size, can be traced back to information coded in our genes. We call that information our *genetics,* and it is written in our DNA. All human bodies have the same types of genes, but the specific information contained in each gene varies. For example, we all have genes for eye color, but some genes contain the information for brown eyes, while others carry blueprints for blue eyes (*blue*prints for *blue* eyes . . . see what I did there?). We inherit our genes from our biological mothers and fathers. At the moment of conception, the female and male genes combine, and *violá*, a new human being is made. Because there's an infinite number of possible genetic combinations, we all look different.

Our unique genetic blueprint is stamped into every cell in our bodies. That's over 200 different types of cells! How does a blood cell know it's a blood cell and not a cell from your tongue or spine? Our bodies are smart. Every cell carries its own recipe for making its structural elements—its building blocks. This recipe is executed by specific proteins and enzymes that activate our genes by attaching themselves to our DNA, causing it to unfold. Maybe you remember the famous double helix (spiral ladder) shape of our DNA? Proteins and enzymes eventually detach from our DNA, which folds back up into its double helix in response. This process of folding and unfolding activates or suppresses certain genes. We call this process *epigenetics*. The proteins of a blood cell "know" they're a blood cell and act accordingly. Fascinating, huh?

Genetics and epigenetics control our physical bodies, everything from our phenotype (how we look) to our hip flexibility and risk for certain diseases.

Our mind and emotions work the same way, according to my research. Each of us are born with a unique set of psychological "genes" that conveys information about how we will go about fulfilling our basic needs for autonomy, competency, and connection.

Like our physical characteristics, our "psychological DNA" has infinite potential combinations. These combinations are expressed as our core values. No two individual's core values are exactly the same. Because our perception of what matters most is necessarily *subjective*, the specific combination of values that best fulfills our psychological needs of autonomy, competence, and connection is unique to each of us. For example, someone may feel autonomous when they purchase a house. Someone else may feel in charge of her life by performing in a community theater during the weekends. For some, autonomy comes from working nine to five, spending a day deep sea fishing, or following their intuition and inner guidance.

OUTSIDE IN: BEAUTIFULLY UNIQUE

As for our physical genes and looks, there's no "right" or "wrong", or most definitely not "perfect" combination. We're all beautifully unique.

Let's check out my core values linked to the basic need for connection. I have friends who are women and friends who are men. I enjoy the company of millennials as well as Generation Xers, baby boomers, and civics. I spend time with academics as well as people who think studying is a waste of time. My favorite people come from different countries. And although my friends are diverse, they all have one thing in common: they enjoy deep conversations. Our visits include discussions that often lead to wild ideas of saving the world. Another thing we share are long-lasting friendships. I have known my friends for ten, sometimes more than twenty, years. This makes perfect sense because the values that matter most to my need for connection are *awareness* and *loyalty*.

My sister and I are wildly different. While I enjoy discussing deep topics preferably on a remote sandy beach, she loves hiking, biking, and attending live events with her favorite people. The more, the merrier. Nothing is more fun for her (and horrifying to me) than a surprise party.

I remember visiting her in Lucca, Italy, where she was studying for her PhD. It was the longest period we'd gone without seeing each other, and I was so happy and excited. I imagined us strolling around the old town, going from one coffee bar to another, sitting in the sun and talking about our past, present, future . . . our hopes, fears, and feelings. And how we would save the world, of course.

She was also excited to host me. She carefully planned my stay in an attempt to make every moment memorable. She organized: 1) two gigantic outdoor parties with all the amazing food you could imagine, great Italian wine, a powerful sound system, and friends ready to sing, dance, and have fun; 2) two whole-day biking trips; 3) a visit to an amateur soccer game; and 4) endless lunches and drinks with people she cared about.

I burst into tears one evening in Lucca, craving more intimate time with my sister. At the same time, she couldn't believe I'd failed to enjoy her plans. She'd undertaken a massive effort to ensure we'd have fun.

For a while, we struggled with our differences. Over the years, we finally realized that what makes relationships work for my sister is different from what makes relationships work for me. I value intimate and one-on-one time with lots of deep conversations; she values external stimulation and sharing her good mood with as many people as possible. The truth is, neither one of us has the "right" way to fulfill our need to connect (but admit it anyway, which team are you on, mine or my sister's?). It's simply that we each hold different sets of values, which determine how we want to connect with the people we most love, and this is as real as having brown hair and a big nose (oh, that's actually me).

"Smooth Criminal"[21]

In an ideal world, we could link all of our external actions and behaviors to our core values. Everything we say and do would be an expression of what matters most to us. But we all know this doesn't happen. In the real world, we often find ourselves behaving in ways that, deep down, feel inauthentic and don't serve our wellbeing. We get stuck in patterns of thinking and behaving in certain ways because we think we *should*. BUT WHY, you ask?

Here's one important difference between our physical genetics and our "psychological DNA:" while it takes a good deal of time, effort, and money to suppress our physical characteristics (think Michael Jackson), it's astonishingly easy to stifle our core values. We're all unconsciously guilty of subduing and censoring our core values because, as it turns out, we aren't running on only one set of values . . . our core values compete for our attention with the external values we pick up along the way—our acquired values.

Thought Experiment: My Core Values

- The Appendix contains a list of values. Take a moment and choose ten to fifteen of the values, those you feel are most important to living a happy, fulfilled life. Feel free to add any values you can't find on the list—no list is complete.

- The traits, which link your posse, will likely be important values you need to build relationships and connect. What differentiates the best close relationships you have from those that are just acquaintances? What is the common denominator between your closest friends?

- The things the people closest to you know and appreciate about you can be a great clue about your top values. Ask your closest friends, "What can't I help but be?" or "What unique features make me, me?" For

---

21   Michael Jackson, "Smooth Criminal." *Bad*. Michael Jackson and Quincy Jones, 1988.

example, I've heard my friends tell me time and again, "I feel so much better after talking to you."

II.

The Roadblocks To Being You

Chapter 3

Your Acquired Values

Let's go back to my *Personal Foundation* class again. Do you remember how my colleagues and I weren't sure of our own values? To help us identify our core values, we were given a long list of potential values—the same list you may have used to complete the thought experiment at the end of Chapter 2 (if you haven't completed it yet, don't wait another moment—it's important). We were tasked with choosing the ten values most important to us, ranking them from the least important to the most-mostest important. It's not as easy as it sounds. Nearly all of us struggle to be brutally honest about our messy, imperfect inner selves.

This became painfully obvious to me when I realized I was the only student in the class who easily and quickly chose my top ten values. I was surprised to see my colleagues agonizing over the assignment, taking twice as long and coming up with only a few words. As the clock ticked on, I studied my classmates, trying to figure out if I'd missed something. Did they know something that I didn't? Had I done the assignment wrong?

Kevin was having a seriously intense reaction. I observed his flushed face and his fidgety hands and, most surprising of all, I watched as he shot furtive glances at his neighbors, checking out which words they had selected. Kevin looked ashamed for peeping at others' work. I couldn't help but think of someone trying to cheat on an exam. But, why? I didn't understand why a class exercise without any right or wrong answers, which only asked us to describe ourselves, would be so uncomfortable. *Take it easy, Kev! Only you know what makes you fulfilled and happy*, I wanted to tell my classmate. *What's the big deal?*

As it turns out, Kevin was afraid of what the rest of us might think of his choices. He worried over choosing the "right" values. Will he look superficial if he chooses *money* or *wealth*? Will people question his masculinity if he chooses *caring* or *kindness*? Shouldn't he choose *achievement* or *productivity*? He's shared a lot about his kids in this class—he probably *should* choose *family*, right?

I had a front row seat to Kevin's internal fight between what matters most to him and what his values *should* be, to avoid ridicule and look good in front of the rest of us. Although I didn't yet have a vocabulary for Kevin's battle, I knew I was witnessing something important.

Realizing what was going on was such an "aha" moment for me. I figured that our core values don't exist in a vacuum—our own understanding of our values is heavily influenced by external pressure and messages. All the advice we've received and messages we've absorbed from others have been coded into our system of values. And what if we can't resist the pressure, like Kevin, and we spend our entire lives constantly choosing between our own values and the values we acquire because we believe we *should* pursue them?

I felt in my gut that I was on to something. Simply reflecting on our life values isn't enough. We have to understand that we have also subconsciously adopted values along the way from outside sources, such as family, teachers, ministers, social media, politics, and pop culture.

Acquired values represent all of the things *our surroundings* tell us we must have or feel to experience autonomy, competency, and connection. Our core values, on the other hand, are the *intrinsic* knowledge we all have about how to best meet our needs. Our acquired values reflect social norms and attitudes and are the things we use to judge or compare ourselves with others. Sometimes, our acquired values serve us well; yet often, they don't.

Furthermore, these acquired values co-exist with our core values. Without this knowledge, we can really mess ourselves up.

GOING VIRAL

To understand our acquired values, let's go back to the concept of "psychological DNA" and consider what happens in our bodies when viruses attack us. Some viruses incorporate their genetic material into our DNA, which allows them to produce more building blocks of the virus, needed for their replication. Spending the nutrients and energy on building more viruses leaves our bodies exhausted and without enough resources to build our own proteins. *This* is why we get sick.

Imagine our acquired values as "viruses" for our psychological DNA. These viruses represent what our outside environment has told us we must do to achieve lasting wellbeing. Like infected cells, we spend time and energy "replicating" values that aren't even our own. We have little left to give to fulfill our goals based on our core values.

The major challenge here is that we're exposed to these viruses when we're young and more susceptible and not aware of our own core values. That's why some of these values are coded into our brains at such a fundamental level that we can't easily bring them to the surface and question their validity. The result, a mosh pit of external values and our own core values, makes it difficult to recognize our original "genes."

ALL I DO IS WIN

I mentioned in Chapter 2 that *motivation* is one of my core values. I could also describe it as the fastest, easiest, and most energy-efficient way for me to feel competent. It's my shortcut to feeling good! In an ideal world, my core value of motivation and the intrinsic power that comes from it would have been noticed early on. My surroundings would have supported me in pursuing *motivation* and encouraged me to choose a career that involves a great deal of motivating others. Well, we all know we don't live in ideal world. And my childhood and adolescence were *un-ideal*. No one noticed I was naturally driven by motivation. Instead, I received the repeated message that there is a "formula" for success:

- Go to a good university (in my family, "good" meant "known for the natural sciences").
- Earn a degree from that university.
- Get that high-paying job (work hard and don't even consider quitting).
- Climb the company ladder.
- Buy a house (and accumulate savings).
- And then you'll feel competent and successful. And happy, of course.

These messages were loud, reinforcing the attitudes and behaviors my family modeled for me. These messages drowned out the quiet voices in my head, the voices that may have served me better. Looking back, it's no surprise that I acquired the value of *academic success.*

I learned at an early age to strive for success. When I was in kindergarten, a local dentist sponsored a drawing contest. I still remember that 156 kids entered artwork. I won! And I was thrilled. But the excitement was short-lived. I felt overwhelmed from the attention I received from my parents, teachers, and friends. Instead of asking to see my award-winning drawing, my friends wanted to see my medal. My young brain absorbed a not-quite-helpful concept:

What you produce is not as important as succeeding.

An acquired value was born.

Of course, there's nothing wrong with wanting to be successful. The problem began when I started to see success as my only path to happiness. I looked outside for validation and did not listen to the whispers of my own intuition. I understand now that my pursuit of success had shades of addiction. I felt good about myself when I won, and then I judged myself and felt ashamed and unworthy when I lost. This happened because I'd aligned myself with my acquired values rather than my core values. It took me twenty years to start controlling my success, as opposed to letting success control me. And it's taken me two decades to actively support my career as a biochemist with projects that serve my number one core value of *motivation.*

Were you nodding along at various parts of my story? I wouldn't be surprised if you were. Most of us can share a similar story about following the subtle suggestions or outright mandates of our environments. And these stories don't always have happy endings. This happens because we haven't yet learned that following our core values, and not the acquired ones, brings us the deepest contentment.

TRULY, MADLY, DEEPLY, GOOD AGAIN

It's hard to shake things up. It's hard to change our lives. At the end of the day, it's often easier to flip on Netflix and zone out. Even when we recognize we aren't living our best lives, giving ourselves permission to do something different doesn't come easy. Without any help from formal education or personal-growth support systems, it takes a whole lot of self-knowledge to recognize acquired values and their false promises.

But I can't tell you enough how worthwhile the work is. Many people I've worked with say one thing over and over again: *I wish I'd understood the concepts of core and acquired values a lot sooner.* If we don't want to keep making decisions based on the values we've adopted, we must train ourselves to separate our core values from our acquired values. Only then will we be able to make choices in service of what matters most. Only then will we feel truly, madly, deeply good again.

CORE OR ACQUIRED?

How do you tell the difference between a core value and an acquired value? Start by considering:

- **Want or Should?** What do you do out of *inspiration*, and what do you do out of a sense of *obligation*? Inspiration makes us feel excited and alive; our bodies feel lighter and more open to All The Good Things. Obligations create stress and tension, which we can feel in knotted muscles, increased blood pressure, and conditions, including anxiety or depression.

- **My Hot List or DJ?** Think of your core values as your favorite music, your all-time greatest hits playlist. When you act on your acquired values, though, you're playing for the crowd. You may hate Today's Top 40, but you play it because it's what others want and expect.

- **Just a Fling or Love of Your Life?** Pursuing our acquired values gives us momentary flashes of happiness that don't last. When the rush is over, we're back looking for our next thrill. In contrast, our core values are here to stay. The positive effects of aligning ourselves with our core values accumulate over time and brings long-lasting happiness.

- **Devil or Angel?** Acquired values are like the devil on our shoulder, constantly whispering into our ear. When we're younger, this voice is external, but over time, our brains internalize and repeat the stories others gave us. Whatever you call those nagging, persistent voices in the back of your mind, it's likely they're telling you that what you do is never enough.

"Ay, Chihuahua!"[22] (a.k.a. the Devil on Your Shoulder)

But, you ask, if our core values are so deeply and intrinsically part of us, why doesn't our reality always naturally reflect our authentic selves?

Check out this illustration.

---

22   Lucha Villa, "Ay, Chihuahua!" *El Relampago*, 1962.

It captures 100 percent my interpretation of the interaction between our core and acquired values. Our acquired values act like the angry, feisty, barking Chihuahua, making up for feeling small by being loud and aggressive. On the other hand, our core values know their own strength and worth; they don't need to bark for attention. They are an inseparable part of us, stable and real. Laid-back and patient, like this Boxer, they simply feel compassion for our acquired values, understanding they're the relics of our ancestry and the necessary illusions of childhood.

Every day our two sets of values compete over our time, energy, and focus. Imagine a situation in which you are trying to take your two dogs, the little Chihuahua and the peaceful Boxer, for a walk. The Boxer represents your passions, your inherent values and yearnings; the little Chihuahua represents your intellect, your acquired values and moral mind. As you approach a fork in the road, the little Chihuahua wants to take a familiar path because the unknown is scary, and the good old way feels safe for him. He gets really loud, pointing out all of the possible and impossible scenarios of what might happen if you don't go the way he wants, the way you've always gone, and the way you should always go. You become anxious that something bad will happen to you if you don't listen. You also know that when you do listen, a burst of dopamine will flood your body, creating relief and spikes of happiness. The Boxer senses your wish to follow the "road less traveled" and engage in different sorts of activities. He's happy to support you along the way but lets you decide. The Boxer understands that for the full experience, *you have to choose for yourself.* But many times, the barking Chihuahua is so quick that you don't even realize you have a choice. You feel as if your only choice would be to revisit the other path with your Boxer later, when you have time, and when you finish what has to be done.

As a dog owner, it is your job to tame the little Chihuahua and guide both dogs to switch between the two paths in the way you willingly choose, the way you truly believe will bring you where you want to be in the long run. In other words, we are constantly pulled in two directions by opposing forces: what we want to do and what we believe we should do. It's up to us to choose how to balance the two in service of our long-term wellbeing, as my friend Donna learned.

STRIVING OR THRIVING—IT'S YOUR CALL

Donna was a lawyer for a while, one of those successful ones who everyone would consider crazy for leaving her well-established career path. As a lawyer, Donna was fulfilling her need for competency by pursuing her acquired values of *status, reputation,* and *prestige,* which did not serve her wellbeing in the long run. Out of curiosity (and to dial down the pressures resulting from her job), she took a class on makeup art, and she loved it so much that within a couple of years, she launched her own beauty school. Today, Donna is such a successful makeup artist that she's booked for months in advance. But most importantly, helping other women look and feel beautiful for their special occasions brings her enormous joy and feelings of competence and contribution. Courageously making the unforeseen leap, Donna discovered that while she did feel successful when working as a lawyer, she felt successful *and* deeply content when pursuing her core values of *art, creativity,* and *empowering women.*

Donna's story shows how when we pursue and seek to fulfill our acquired values, we can find ourselves in suboptimal situations. Let's go back to our apple tree from Chapter 2. Earlier, we saw how our values are rooted in our basic needs, and our behaviors and actions grow out of our values. In a healthy "tree," our behaviors align with our core values, and we bear fruit.

Now, it's time to complicate the story . . . When we want to fulfill our basic needs, we actually have two options: activate the core values coded into our "psychological DNA" or strive to meet others' expectations. When we follow our core values, we flourish. When we choose to follow our acquired values, we can find ourselves withering, unable to maintain our wellbeing. The good news for us, unlike trees, is that when we find ourselves wilting, we can *choose* to do things differently (sorry, trees). Like Donna, we can branch out on our own and blossom.

DEAD WEIGHT FOR ME, APPLES FOR YOU

Here's something I found out during my research that I still can't get over: one person's acquired value can be another's core value and vice versa. It's fascinating to watch how different people engage differently with the same concept.

Iris struggled with her appearance for most of her childhood. Obese and Dumbo-eared, the other kids made fun of her. This constant teasing made her see (and acquire) the value *appearance* as the ultimate way to create connections. In high school, she lost A LOT of weight. Her first boyfriend praised her physical beauty, reinforcing her acquired value. I watched how Iris changed from the curious girl I knew into a young woman who went to extremes to maintain her physical appearance. Her desire to appear physically perfect became an obsession, an unhealthy one. As she neglected her true interests, she stopped thriving. As her friend, I could see a deep unhappiness beneath the muscle-toned and slender surface.

Like all of us, Iris wanted to create meaningful relationships, and her early life experience showed her that focusing on her appearance could provide those connections. Iris's choices worked to some extent. She *was* able to transform her body and create relationships. But, if she was honest with herself, her adopted lifestyle and the kind of people that came with it weren't bringing her fulfillment. Her behaviors of "extreme exercising" or being "good-looking" attracted the kind of people who also found these things important (people like her ex-boyfriend), making her feel as if she had no choice but to keep up her attractiveness.

For Iris, the acquired value of *appearance* didn't work out for her in the way she'd hoped.

Charlotte, however, thrives when she focuses on *appearance*. It's one of her core values and brings her a lot of joy. At six feet tall (183 cm for my European readers), Charlotte towered over her peers in high school. Instead of feeling like a freak, she took pride in her crazy long legs by wearing brightly patterned leggings. Now an adult, Charlotte works as a speech therapist for kids. But in her spare time, she and her boyfriend attend cosplay parties where they dress in elaborate, sometimes whacky, costumes. They love to go to ComicCon every year, dressed as their favorite characters. Charlotte still loves to wear bright colors and sequins, and she still allows her playful side to show in the way she dresses. In fact, her ability to embrace an appearance that some find silly serves her well in her job with kids with special needs. Kids are drawn to Charlotte's confidence and her colorful style, and she finds it easy to establish the trust she needs with her students to provide the best therapy. In both her private and professional life, Charlotte's playful approach to her appearance brings her enormous joy and a feeling of competence and contribution. So, while the value of appearance may feel like dead weight for Iris; for Charlotte, this value bears fruit.[23]

TAKE IT EASY, PLEASE

I shared before that I was (still am) super excited when I discovered we all have core *and* acquired values and that what's a core value for someone may be an acquired for others. Maybe you're with me on this. Perhaps you're also feeling energized by this new knowledge; maybe you feel as if a heavy weight has finally been lifted. But not everyone feels this way. Some people feel confused. They wonder if they know themselves at all and feel uncertain about how to move forward. And then there are some of us, like my friend Jenni, impatient and ready to take bold action immediately. If she were here, she'd say, *I want to make dramatic changes, and I want to start making them NOW—right this minute.*

And if Jenni were here, I'd lovingly tell her to take it easy. We often set ourselves up to fail by initiating change that is too great. Getting rid of our acquired values ASAP isn't the goal here. Our acquired values are neither good nor bad *per se*; we just need to understand if they're taking *too much* of our time, energy, and efforts. In the following chapters, I'll show you how to recognize when, where, and how your acquired values might be standing in the way of your own success and wellbeing. Instead of seeking drastic change, I hope you'll embrace my proven-to work strategy to generate exciting results *over time.*

---

23   Status Update: While writing this chapter and thinking back on my friend Iris, I surrendered to my curiosity and Googled her. It had been twenty years since we last had contact, and I was excited to find out how her life was unfolding. *Et voilà.* I found her happy face on the Faculty List of a very prestigious research university. True Iris is back, scoring a little victory in the core versus acquired values faceoff. Yay!

Thought Experiment: I Think You Should . . .

- In a journal, write down one to three messages you received from your parents about how you "should" behave or what you "should" achieve in life.
- Notice how you are feeling emotionally when you think about those *shoulds*. Write that down, too.
- Now pay attention to your body. What's going on? How's it different from how you felt when thinking about your favorite activities at the end of Chapter 2?
- Using the list of values in the Appendix, consider which values are at the heart of your *shoulds*. For example, if your parents urged you to earn good grades, *status, education,* or *achievement* might be values that are the foundation for that advice. Write down at least three values for each piece of advice.
- If you felt drained, heavy, or constricted as you thought about your *shoulds*, it's likely the values attached to those messages are acquired. In contrast, we feel lighter and more animated when we consider our core values. Remember, clearly recognizing our acquired values gives us the opportunity to choose to keep them or to let them go.

Chapter 4

Three Ways Acquired Values Trip Us Up

One July afternoon, my kids and I were enjoying an ice cream at our favorite café when I overheard a couple having an uncomfortable conversation. Just as I was spooning my first bite of salted caramel brownie into my mouth, the woman stood up abruptly, tossed a few Euros on the table, and said to her companion loudly, "I'm so sick of how you keep *saying* one thing but *doing* another!" She stormed off (before I could give her my card and recommend she try some coaching).

Perhaps unknowingly, this woman had put her finger on one of the biggest ways our acquired values can trip us up. We can experience internal tension when our actions don't match our words (which is what this woman was so angry about). I often think of this couple and wonder what sparked their argument. What was her companion saying, and why didn't his actions match his words? Was he telling her he cared about her dog, Slippers, but always finding ways to get out of walking him? Maybe he'd claimed to love outdoor sports but couldn't commit to booking a trekking holiday with her? Who knows.

I wish I could've sat down with that couple and shared with them what I *do* know and what my research proves—we experience tension when there's a mismatch between what we *say* is important and what we actually *do*. Researchers call this discrepancy **the Rhetoric-Reality Gap.** Individuals can feel the friction of a Rhetoric-Reality Gap and so can organizations and even countries. The Rhetoric-Reality Gap is one of the three ways our acquired values can trip us up.

1. THE RHETORIC-REALITY GAP

While we'll never know what my ice cream couple clashed over, Reyna's story offers a clear example of a mismatch between words and deeds. Reyna *says* her perfect Sunday morning involves brunching with friends or meditating in the park, yet most Sundays find her working on the data analyses she didn't complete on Friday. Later, she feels sad for not joining her friends but convinces herself that it was *just* this weekend, it was an absolute exception—necessary for optimal progress in her PhD. She also promises herself that she will go next weekend to make-up for it.

It turns out that working non-stop is something Reyna thinks she *should* do because of how she was raised. She picked up an acquired value from her family, who emphasized *hard work* and *dedication* as the only "right" path to success, while at the same time, considered taking time off as laziness. In reality, Reyna stays home, absorbed by her excel sheets, rather than experiencing connection with her friends over waffles or with her higher power while meditating outdoors, behaviors aligned with her core values of *community*, *spirituality*, and *nature*. The gap between what she *says* matters to her and what she chooses to do is a classic Rhetoric-Reality Gap.

There's nothing fundamentally "wrong" or "bad" about experiencing a Rhetoric-Reality Gap. In fact, such moments are like road signs pointing to our core and acquired values. What's important is the understanding that, sometimes, these values will clash and create friction. Without the vocabulary of core versus acquired values, we can't recognize a value we've adopted along the way, and we're at greater risk of frustration and disappointment.

But when we train ourselves to pay attention to a Rhetoric-Reality Gap, we can tune into the information about ourselves, which these moments convey. With that information, we can choose to act in stronger alignment with our core values.

That's Not Really How I Got Ya

My parents are prouder if I get good grades in my classes than if I'm a caring community member in class and school. Agree or disagree? Does this statement represent your childhood? What about your own kids—would they agree or disagree?

Researchers Rick Weissbourd and Stephanie Jones from the Harvard Graduate School of Education asked this question to hundreds of kids.[24] You may be surprised that the children in the study overwhelming agreed that their parents are prouder of their good grades than their caring behavior by a margin of four to one. The parents were certainly surprised—they had all *said* that instilling kindness and care for others was their top parenting priority. Yet, the children's words demonstrated value for achievement and personal success over a concern for others.

The graphic on the next page illustrates what Weissbourd and Jones concluded—that there's a gap between the values parents say matter most and the values their children actually hear, internalize, and demonstrate. In other words, what we say is important to us as adults is not always reflected in how we raise our kids.

Failed parenting? Selfish kids? Nope. The mismatch begins with a gap between parents' core and acquired values. Without a clear understanding of their own values, these parents experienced a gap between what they *say* are their top priorities and what messages their day-to-day behaviors *convey*.

Work to Love or Love to Work?

My own research also points to a Rhetoric-Reality Gap between what we say we care about and how we spend our time. In 2015, I conducted a survey with adults in both the United States and Germany. I asked participants ten questions, including in which area of life they most wanted to succeed. The top choice for people in both countries was *love and relationships*. We do love being in love and being well connected to our friends and family. I also asked people

---

24 "The Children We Mean to Raise: The Real Messages Adults Are Sending About Values." Making Caring Common Project, Harvard Graduate School of Education, July 2014, accessed 10 Feb 20201, https://mcc.gse.harvard.edu/reports/children-mean-raise.

RHETORIC-REALITY GAP

about which area of life receives most of their time and energy—and most chose *career*. The graph below shows that in the United States, only around 15 percent of the participants said they put most of their effort into successful *love and relationships*.

My participants' answers revealed a discrepancy between what they say they prioritize and how they actually spend their time and energy.

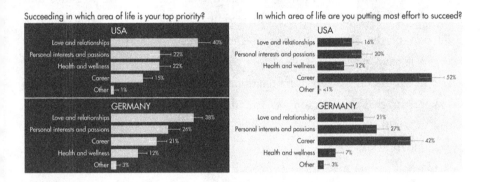

Baloney Wedding

I was seven years old when I first figured out that what people say matters and what people actually do aren't always the same.

Two years earlier, I had attended the wedding of a close family friend. It was the first wedding I'd ever been to, and I was enchanted by the white roses, balloons, and fancy dresses. The bride, Nadia, the daughter of my dad's friend, had dated the groom, Dario, for twelve years before finally deciding to marry. I remember listening to them share the vows they'd written for each other. It was a fairy tale come true right before my five-year-old eyes.

Until it wasn't. Nadia and Dario divorced two years later. Upset and confused, I asked my mom what happened. I didn't really understand my mother's response. She said a lot of things: *Sometimes people grow apart. People change. They just weren't compatible anymore. People have different opinions, and they can't resolve the conflict.* And the one I hated the most: *You'll understand when you're older.*

It had never occurred to me that people could so passionately celebrate their love and still be unhappy. Aren't weddings the happy ending we all want?

Many years later, I learned the truth. Family, friends, and culture had been bombarding Nadia and Dario with messages about the importance of getting married. *When are you getting married? If you split up now, after all those years, you'll never make up for lost time. It's time for you to marry and have a family. You won't feel fulfilled without marriage and a family.*

Looking back as an adult, married and with a family of my own, I can imagine how hard they must've worked to conform to social pressures and maintain appearances. The beautiful wedding I attended (the reality) was a reflection of the acquired baloney beliefs played out in their minds: *being married is most important.* The instinct coming from their hearts (the rhetoric) was different—being in a healthy relationship matters more than being married. As they struggled to maintain the "shoulds" their wedding symbolized, Nadia and Dario stifled their doubts about their compatibility until they finally parted ways, unhappy and spent.

If I had a time machine, I'd go back in time and share what I now know with Nadia and Dario. I'd help them differentiate between their core and their acquired values and help them identify how their acquired values weren't serving them. I'd help them to see—and appreciate—the gap between what really matters to them and how they act. I'd remind them that when we identify a gap between our rhetoric and our reality, we're in a stronger position to focus on our core values and find genuine fulfillment.

Practice, Not Perfect

I've thought about these concepts for decades, and I understand my own values well. But even I don't experience a 100 percent alignment between my rhetoric and my reality. And I'm okay with that.

It's common for adults to have a large gap between their rhetoric and their realities. In my value study (as I like to call it), participants frequently discovered their actions aligned with their core values less than 50 percent of the time. I assured them—as I assure myself and as I assure you—it's normal to discover that the gap between our rhetoric and our reality is bigger than we expect. *Being you* isn't about achieving a perfect match between your core values and your behavior. Shrinking the gap over time is the best part of our journey.

As I grow older, it becomes easier to reduce my chances of experiencing a Rhetoric-Reality Gap. Now that I'm a parent, my free time is precious. Having kids has shown me how valuable my time is and has forced me to pay attention to what I do with those special moments. I'm more mindful of how I spend those precious hours, and I'm razor-focused on aligning it with my core values.

But I'm still not perfect, and I doubt I ever will be. I'm grateful for those moments of mismatch because they remind me—by clearly recognizing the Rhetoric-Reality Gap—I've just taken the first step to reclaiming my core values. If you give it a try, it'll rock your world, I promise.

2. THE NEW YEAR'S RESOLUTION PARADOX

The anticipation. The parties. The glitter of silver and gold. Concerts. TV specials. The glasses, filled with something fizzy, raised to our family and friends . . . or maybe to ourselves. And of course, the countdown: *10, 9, 8 . . .* Ah, the bitter sweetness of saying good-bye to one year and welcoming in a new year.

But what would New Year's be without our resolutions? Earnest commitment or party joke, many of us seize the opening of the calendar year to make new goals or new commitments to goals we've been neglecting.

As I write this book, my friend Li has been preparing for a big move. While going through some old, neglected boxes from her university days, she found a list of her New Year's resolutions, nearly two decades old. She was ruefully delighted to notice she never accomplished any of the things her younger self had set out to do, and, what's more, she had to admit that she'd probably list many of those same goals on her resolutions list this year. Li laughed, posting a picture of her perpetually unfulfilled goals on her social media pages.

Li's discovery underscores an incredibly common aspect of human behavior. We like to make goals and are even pretty darn good at it. Studies show, in fact, that 50 percent of people in the US make New Year's resolutions. Yet, we often aren't quite as good at actually following through on the vows we so determinedly made.

In the two weeks that follow, we dedicate ourselves to our goals. We hit the gym, volunteer at the community center, reduce our carbs, and squirrel away an extra dollar here and there. So far, so good. Alas, by the time Valentine's Day rolls around, many of us are backsliding (chocoooooolate!). By July? Forget about it. Less than half of us are sticking to our resolutions. By December, 90 percent of us are, like Li, back where we started. Rinse. Repeat. Researchers did the math and found that 88 percent of all resolutions fail.[25] That's 150 million people with billions of regrets and self-imposed guilt trips.

> *"Decided my New Year starts again on February 1st. This was a trial month."*
> —Anonymous

Look Before You Leap

But what about that 10 percent of folks who DO manage effective change? James Prochaska and Carlo Di Clemente took a look at people who accomplish their goals and found successful people actually experience six different stages of change.[26] Instead of making big changes all at once (a message found everywhere in our culture), the researchers discovered that we're more likely to be successful when we take our time and tackle those goals step-by-step. At the heart of our struggle to stick-to-it may be a lack of preparation. We jump into making resolutions before we are ready.

I've also found this to be true in my own research. It's worth it to take a pause before rushing into big decisions to ask ourselves if what we're reaching for is aligned with our core values or with those outside voices telling us what we *should* want/be/do. When we consciously choose a plan of action focused on our core values, we're much more likely to stick to the plan and more likely to feel satisfied and fulfilled.

Engage Your Core (Values)!

I smiled when I heard my friend Li's story of failed resolutions because I could relate. We laughed and agreed: When your New Year's resolution hits its tenth anniversary, maybe it's time to reconsider your perspective.

---

25 http://www.richardwiseman.com/quirkology/new/USA/Experiment_resolution.shtml
26 Prochaska, J.O. and DiClemente, C.C. "Stages and Processes of Self-Change of Smoking: Toward an Integrative Model of Change." *Journal of Consulting and Clinical Psychology*, 1983.

During my two pregnancies, I gained weight. Those extra pounds (or kilos) didn't magically disappear as I left the hospital with my youngest in my arms. Eventually, my mom, usually helpful and kind, noticed that my squishiness wasn't going anywhere.

"Enough time has passed. It's time to get in shape," she said. "Your problem," she went on to say, "is that you're happy whether you're ten kilos overweight or 10 kilos underweight."

And she's right. I wasn't as worried about my weight as she wanted me to be. But I also wasn't blind, either. I tried to lose the weight. Repeatedly. My resolution didn't extend only to New Year's but also on Valentine's Day, my birthday, Easter, Halloween, you name the holiday, and I tried. I even joined a program for new moms at the gym and did my best to restore those core muscles. I *hated* it. I realized that I had made fitness about my *appearance* instead of my overall wellbeing, and I was completely unmotivated as a result.

Today, I don't "work out." But I do have fun moving my body because I link physical activity to my core values. I bike to work not to slim down but because it neatly fits my schedule (right before and right after work), offering the perfect length of time (twenty-five minutes each way) to practice mindfulness. By doing this, I'm activating my core values of *awareness* and *presence*. I also play table tennis in an amateur league. This appeals to another core value of mine, *achievement*. And when my little ones join those activities, they become the ultimate joy, supporting another top core value—*family*.

If I haven't chosen to engage my core values instead of following my fitness teacher's mandate—*engage your core!*—none of what now works flawlessly for me would have been possible.

To School for Cool

I've been on both edges of a social (dis)approval spectrum. I was hopelessly uncool as a kid. Other kids, the "cool" kids, teased me about the clothes I wore (the combination of white sport socks and black leather shoes was the big one) and the hairstyle I had (it's hard to explain, you'd have to see it). Even my mom pressured me to tame my wild hair for the yearbook pictures. Being perfectly nerdy, I was happiest when I was studying chemistry, reading a good book, or playing ping pong—and not worrying about my appearance.

I thought I would never turn out to be cool, and, miraculously, I was on good terms with this fact. But then, almost overnight, clothes weren't important anymore—graduating from university was, and, out of blue, I started being cool in the new world order. I found it incredibly interesting that some of the "cool" kids from my school kept adding me on social media and starting conversations that would have never ever happened some years before. And just as I was getting used to it, desirable values were swapped again.

When starting family and accumulating wealth emerged as new markers of success, I was earning a PhD, followed by years of postdoc (my fellow comrades laugh now). It's probably the worst career choice if you want to achieve wealth and start a family: earning a relatively poor wage, expected to relocate many times, even on different continents (which will definitely bury your budget and decrease your chances of a stable relationship), all while working long hours where you have no real "time off," no real "weekends." During those times, I was told by not one, not two, but three different people that everything I had accomplished up until this point in my life (including my degrees, winning a national team championship in table tennis, living in three different countries, pursuing a scientific project I'm passionate about, and marrying an awesome guy) no longer mattered unless I had kids.

I was swimming with, and I was swimming against, what society wants, and I can tell you this: when your values and interests are aligned with what society values, things are easy for you. You don't need to waste mental energy to fight the outside forces. But, when your personal interests and values drift away from what is socially desired, you enter a not-so-friendly zone and things are more difficult. It is no surprise to me that so many people crack under the societal pressure and try to align themselves with socially desirable acquired values, unfortunately not understanding that this is the quickest way for their resolutions to fail.

3. NOT IN THE CARDS

At every stage of our lives, we make decisions with which our future selves are not always thrilled. As adults, we may endure the pain of removing the very tattoos that, as youngsters, we boasted on our biceps. We may divorce the person who, once upon a time, we were dying to marry. We may regret our career paths—the same ones we were ready to sacrifice for. As it turns out, we are very bad predictors of own futures and our future selves. Unless you're a bona fide fortuneteller, it's likely you've had some experience with things not working out the way you thought they would.

Why do we make decisions that our future selves often lament?

You guessed it. Not understanding our core and acquired values plays a role in regret. Unlike our stable core values, our acquired values change dramatically over time because the measures of our successes and failures change with each new stage of our lives. This means that for most of our lives we over-strive for the opportunity to indulge our current—acquired—values because we overestimate their stability.

Our journey from craving "likes" on social media to pursuing our ultimate dreams reveals dramatic change over time, with our success measured by different standards. When we're younger, the expectations of others create a heavy weight on our shoulders, and we feel obliged to fulfill them. We set ourselves up to make choices, which our older selves regret. In later life, however, we're nearing our truest selves, trying to make up for the times when we followed the herd instead of blazing our own trails.

"Story of My Life" [27]

Let's break this down and take a closer look at what society deems as signs of success during the five phases of our adult life:

Stage 1: Adolescence

As teens, we're heavily influenced by our peers, social media, and TV. What do these sources glorify as most desirable? Being *trendy*, *good-looking*, *popular*, and *rich*. Are you surprised that over 80 percent of young millennials have reported that their major life goal is to get rich? And another 50 percent said that becoming famous was another major life goal. These values encourage

---

27 One Direction. "Story of My Life." *Midnight Memories*. Syco Music and Columbia Records, 2013.

corresponding behaviors: owning the newest smartphone, sporting top brand clothes, or craving social media likes and followers, for example. We evaluate ourselves and our peers based on the extent to which we meet such expectations. The result? We end up branded as either cool . . . or a loser.

Stage 2: Young Adulthood

Just as we've found out how to be one of the cool kids or accept/embrace our loser status, we find ourselves in the next stage of life, saddled with a whole new set of values by which society will evaluate us. In young adulthood, we meet the pressure to get a degree, acquire a good job, travel the world, be fit, buy a car, and perhaps buy a house or move to the trendiest part of the city. We don't give ourselves a lot of wiggle room. If we don't graduate on time (or at all), we feel the shame of disappointing our family. If we don't transform the world with our first job, we question our own abilities. At a time when we need resilience and grit, society defines success as *achievement, adventure, status, independence, joy,* and *freedom.* And you end up either successful . . . or a loser.

Stage 3: Full Adulthood

It's time to settle down, get serious, take responsibility . . . blah, blah, blah. Some of us figure out how to meet these demands and we land that job, on schedule. Others may be on their own timelines, constantly anxious they've gone off track. Either way, when we enter full adulthood, society updates the requirements—again. We're no longer supposed to value independence and freedom; instead, it's time for *family, responsibility, devotedness, respect* and *wealth* to become our priorities.

And things here get even trickier. We're forced to reckon with society's judgment on how well we've met one or both of two major social mandates: having a family or having a lucrative career. We've typically had to choose to devote our time to one over the other. Depending on what we choose, we face toxic voices of judgment: your life is worthless without a family (with kids preferably); not having a stellar career makes you a human of second order. In this stage, gender plays into how we're perceived by society. Women carry a larger burden of expectation when it comes to having a family, and experience more judgment if they fail to produce a kid or two, while men experience greater social pressure to accumulate wealth and are judged harshly if they do not.

On top of this already impossible scenario, we now have the added pressure of "not having to choose" between having a family *and* that first-rate career *and* lots of money. Those who are *perceived* as being successful at it ALL are society's heroes. We sing their praises, even as our champions may be downing anti-depressants or walking on the edge of burnout. And you end up as either the mighty superhero of the modern world . . . or a loser.

Stage 4: Midlife

A major turning point arrives in midlife, once the children begin to leave the nest. Until this point, we have followed the scripted path dictated by society. We grew up, were educated, found a job, settled down, and started a family. But now, as the pressures of career building and child-rearing ease up, a new situation confronts us. The voices of our acquired values, thrust upon us by society, start to decrease. They retire! Perhaps for the very first time, we start to ponder the true meaning of our lives. We "declutter" our life. We stop doing the things we never really enjoyed, jettisoning our "frenemies" in favor of more time with our closest friends and family.

As we begin to re-prioritize our lives, society's focus shifts from us to our kids, who are about to endure the pressure we just survived. We are relegated to society's backseat, and the only remaining criteria by which we're judged is whether or not our kids are on the "right" path, heading toward college, a job, and a family of their own. The values from the previous decade, such as *family* and *responsibility*, transform into values such as *legacy* and *tradition*.

Stage 5: Late Adulthood

Late adulthood brings a sad but true scenario—society doesn't care much about us anymore. On the bright side, we face fewer judgments from society. In our golden years, we are either nagging, purposeless fools, or wise Yodas, which may not bother us at all. In this stage, the pursuit of *our* dreams becomes more important than anything else, fueled by the desire to leave our mark on the world. After retirement, many of us make important *self-endorsed* contributions to society, and our wisdom and foresight contribute to its advancement.

Didn't See THAT Coming

The idea that our values and priorities shift as we progress through life may seem obvious, but an exciting study by Dan Gilbert and his team at Harvard's Department of Psychology discovered that we actually *underestimate* our ability for future change until we reach our mid-50s.[28] When asked whether they changed a lot in the past ten years and whether they'll change again over the next ten years, adults overwhelmingly answered "yes" to the first question and "no" to the second. Only in hindsight do we realize how much change happens in a decade.

But once we hit older middle age, we *do* change less. And this makes sense when we remember that social pressures and expectations ease up during those years and we naturally reconnect with what matters most.

"THE END OF CHANGE" ILLUSION

MY VALUES CHANGED TREMENDOUSLY IN THE LAST 10 YEARS.

NO, THEY WILL NOT CHANGE MUCH IN THE NEXT 10 YEARS.

---

28 Quoidbach, Jordi, Gilbert, Daniel T., and Timothy D. Wilson. "The End of History Illusion." *Science*, 2013.

A lack of awareness around our core and acquired values explains the discrepancy between how little we expect to change in the future and how much we agree we've changed over time. When we can't distinguish what matters most from what society expects from us, we can't chart a true course by our core values during the shifting tides of society's expectations.

When we learn to embrace our core values earlier in life, we mobilize the courage to embark on our journeys, even though we know we'll surely disappoint someone. Chances are, though, we won't disappoint our future selves.

THE BIG REVEAL

When we design an action plan based on our stable, nurturing core values, fully aware of those giant, shape-shifting neon distractions, chances are we'll close our Rhetoric-Reality Gaps, stick to our plans, and reach our golden years free of regrets.

When I coach people, we (counter intuitively) first talk about their acquired values. There are so many metaphors—gardening, sculpting, hydraulics, weather, art restoration, even skin care—to describe the process of exposing authentic beauty by removing what's getting in the way. Because that's how it works. Before we can reconnect with our core values—our original "psychological DNA"—we have to recognize and deal with those acquired values that might be preventing us from experiencing the joy and fulfillment of what matters most on a daily basis.

I've personally witnessed this exciting process more than several hundred times by now. It is an extraordinary transformation, and I can't wait to share it with you.

Are you ready to figure out your own acquired values? Where did they come from, anyway?

III.

Where Do Our Acquired Values Come from, Anyway?

Chapter 5

Our Immediate Influencers— Family and Close Friends

This is a story a friend once told me:

It was summer, and my parents came to visit us in a beautiful beach town. We enjoyed the warm weather, riding bicycles, eating ice cream and fish dinners, and, of course, spending hours on the beach. The beach is a fascinating laboratory for the study of human behavior—especially a popular, crowded European beach at the height of the summer holidays.

One family in particular caught our eyes. The parents were not old, but also not young, and several small children shouted and laughed and cried and built sandcastles around their beach chairs. The parents were involved in conversations with each other, paying only scant attention to the children. One toddler-sized boy kept throwing handfuls of sand at his father, trying to get his attention. His father ignored him. But the boy continued to shower the adults with sand. And his father continued to ignore him. The boy continued to throw sand. Finally, the father turned toward his son and calmly, but seriously, told him, "Etienne, you have to learn how to play on your own."

I'll never forget what my mother said as she watched this scene unfold: "Well, that kid is well on his way to learning that doing things alone is the ultimate virtue."

When I heard this story, I knew exactly what my friend's mother had meant. She meant that Etienne was learning to value *independence, strength,* and *self-reliance.* What's bad about that, you say? Maybe nothing. Maybe Etienne will grow up to be someone who works well without direction or immediate supervision, a coworker you can trust to get the job done. But if Etienne continues to hear the message that fending for yourself matters more than connecting with others, and if he brings that lesson, unexamined, into his adult life, he may become a person who is unable to ask for help. He may feel that expressing and communicating his needs is a sign of weakness, setting himself up for conflict at work and in his relationships.

Although we may not be aware of the subtle ways our environment affects us until later in life, from the moment of our birth, our environment constantly teaches us what to value. My research suggests that we pick up our acquired values from three main sources: **our microenvironment, our generation,** and **our culture/nation.** Each source forms a layer, built upon and around our core values, beginning with our families and moving outward to our peer group and larger social contexts.

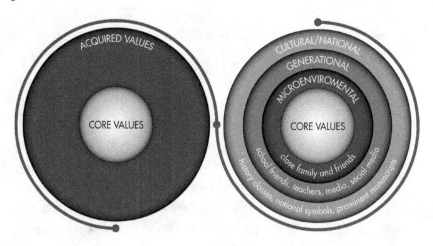

ALL IN THE FAMILY

The strongest influences on our value system—for most of us—are our parents or guardians and our siblings and closest friends. Studies show that parents and guardians are the main influence on their children until age twelve, and it is from them, we all receive our first acquired values, consciously and unconsciously.

Our parents (or primary caregivers) send us messages about what success in life should look like. Maybe it's a college degree, becoming a doctor or a lawyer, or getting married. They also let us know what to avoid if we want to secure our success—seeing a therapist (*you should never show your weaknesses*), filing for divorce (*what will the neighbors say?*), or dating someone of the same sex (*what I just said*). In most cases, our parents don't set out to confuse us or make us miserable. They've found a recipe for happiness in the ingredients on hand—their own core values and the acquired values *they* absorbed from *their* environments. We can benefit from some of their advice, and some of it won't serve us.

When we're young, we don't yet have the wisdom to discern what's useful and what isn't. We aren't old enough to fulfill our own basic needs for personal autonomy, competence, and connection, so we rely on parents or caregivers. Like sponges, we soak up the values we see and hear from our parents and act in ways to win their approval. Our survival depends on it.

A lot of stuff comes up when I help people identify their acquired values— some of it ugly, some of it beautiful, and all of it important information about how we perceive ourselves and the world. Most people recall a specific moment in childhood or adolescence that, in retrospect, they can identify as the source of an acquired value. Words spoken by family members or close friends can haunt us for decades, skewing our thinking and leading us away from our core values.

DEAD-HEADING

Despite what centuries of philosophers and natural scientists believed, we aren't born with a "blank slate;" our brains are not empty vessels waiting to be filled. Exactly the opposite—the human brain is a grand finale of biological engineering. In the process of maturing during pregnancy, the miniature neural tube of only three millimeters in size must expand at an astonishing rate: 250,000 new brain cells every minute (!) to reach 100 billion neurons that fire in a healthy baby brain.[29] Our brains are more than up and running at birth; they're ready-

---

29   Sandra Ackerman. *Discovering the Brain*. Washington, DC: National Academies Press, 1992.

made to adapt to any possible situation we might encounter as newborns and infants.

Part of a newborn brain's ability to adapt involves selecting which connections should stay in the brain (useful stuff) and which connections are lost (not useful stuff). The fancy term for this process is "synaptic pruning." Early on, our genes determine which synapses stay and which go. But, as we grow, synaptic pruning depends upon our experiences. Between ages two and ten, our brains conduct synaptic pruning quickly, grooming our brains for our particular circumstances and personal situations. During our adolescence and twenties, this process slows down. Still, constant stimulation causes synapses to grow and become permanent, all the way into our thirties, making the process of acquiring values powerful indeed.

LET THE APPLE FALL FAR FROM THE TREE

No matter our age, we're wired to enjoy the greatest success when we're motivated from within. We feel fulfilled and driven when we align our core values with our basic psychological needs of autonomy, competence, and connection. There's no better proof of this than kids. Children are naturally curious, highly engaged, creative, physically active, and deeply social beings.

Unless . . .

Unless their parents let their own unfulfilled dreams, judgments, or expectations get in the way.

While there are exceptions (watch this space), we acquire many of our values gradually, during repeated interactions with our parents. In well-meaning attempts to shape their children, parents may be blinded by their own hopes and beliefs. We wish the best for our kids—no doubt about that. Yet we can forget that our kids are not us. It's incredibly hard to let go of this as a parent (I'm guilty, too, I can admit, of wanting my kids to love Ping-Pong as much as I do).

TV and movies, famous books, and even jokes, have popularized the destined-for-tragedy tale of the parent who tries to remake herself in the image of her child and the child who suffers and rebels in response. It's a plotline that's become cliché. Cliché or not, the story has important information for us on the nature of acquired values.

On the one hand, there's a parent who honestly believes they know what's best for their kid, and on the other, a child learning that in order to please their parents and be loved, they must (or at least be seen to) pursue certain values. Parents' hopes, beliefs, and expectations bury their children's intrinsic motivations beneath layers of parental approval and social expectations. Many of us need look no further than our own childhoods to see what a lose-lose situation we can create when we don't understand our acquired values. Disappointed and angry parents and unhappy kids who become unhappy teenagers who become unhappy adults. Can you imagine what your childhood might've been like if your parents had put as much energy into helping you bolster your intrinsic motivations as they did trying to kit you out with all the tools (and even weapons) they thought you needed to be successful? Lesson to parents: Let the apple fall far from the tree.

Boys Don't Cry

What piece of advice from your parents has stuck with you the most?

I'll let you in on one of my secrets: the question above is my fast track to helping people identify their acquired values. How we answer this one question tells us so much about how our parents and family influenced our values. Check out the graphic below. I've collected some responses I've heard from folks and grouped them by topic.

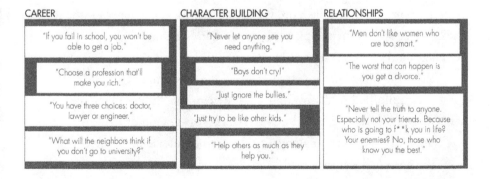

CAREER	CHARACTER BUILDING	RELATIONSHIPS
"If you fail in school, you won't be able to get a job."	"Never let anyone see you need anything."	"Men don't like women who are too smart."
"Choose a profession that'll make you rich."	"Boys don't cry!"	"The worst that can happen is you get a divorce."
"You have three choices: doctor, lawyer or engineer."	"Just ignore the bullies."	"Never tell the truth to anyone. Especially not your friends. Because who is going to f**k you in life? Your enemies? No, those who know you the best."
	"Just try to be like other kids."	
"What will the neighbors think if you don't go to university?"	"Help others as much as they help you."	

Imagine being the child on the receiving end of this advice. What would you learn to value if you repeatedly heard those words?

Throughout his childhood, time and time again, Luke heard, "Boys don't cry." When his mother ended up in the hospital, his entire family told him: "Boys don't cry." He internalized this powerful mantra and learned to bottle up his emotions. He learned quickly that men should not express sadness, grief, anxiety . . . any emotion that might be perceived as "weak." He became "tough." He became so "tough" that when his wife miscarried, he appeared to have no emotional reaction at all. He was so stoic that he failed to provide his wife with the empathy and emotional support she needed during the tragedy. In fact, they almost divorced as a result of Luke's inability to express his emotions.

Our parents have values just like we do. And, just like us, some of their values serve them, and some of them don't. As adults, we can see our parents for what they are—individuals, like us, trying to live their best lives. Some succeed and some still have some work to do. We can choose whether or not to hold onto the values we received from our parents. Because when we don't make such conscious choices, we're likely to end up like the mom in the Easter Ham Story.

THE STORY OF THE EASTER HAM

Every year, Sara watches as her mom cuts off both ends of the Easter ham before putting it on the stove.

"Why do you do that?" Sara asks.

"I don't know. That's the way my mom always prepared the ham."

"But why?"

Her mom sets down the ham, washes her hands, and reaches for the phone. She calls her own mom and puts her on speakerphone in the kitchen. Sara hears her grandmother say she doesn't know.

"That's the way my mom always did it," she says simply.

Now committed to discovering the source of the "Easter Ham Technique," Sara's mom calls her own grandmother, Sara's great-grandmother.

"Grandma, why do you always cut the ends off of a ham before cooking it?"

"The pot I had was too small." she says, laughing.

OK, you might have heard that story before, but it vividly illustrates the point I want to emphasize to you: values that may have mattered to our family in the past don't necessarily matter now. While some values and traditions are worth holding on to and passing along, others might be remnants of old circumstances. The mandate to "clean your plate before you leave the table" may have mattered when money was tight and food was scarce, but now we might recognize the importance of letting children decide for themselves when and how much to eat. On a grander scale, we might've even sacrificed a dream of having our own company or backpacking through Asia after college or pursuing an arts degree to the values of security and modesty held by our parents or grandparents. But we forget that our grandparents lived during or right after the Great Depression or World War II, and their focus was on playing it safe in an unsafe world.

BIG LITTLE TRAUMAS

While we acquire most of our values over time, we can quickly adopt values under fire, when we experience emotionally intense situations. This happens more frequently when we're kids, because our prefrontal brains don't mature until we're seventeen. For us non-neuroscientists or psychologists, this means we're not great at complex thinking patterns, such as putting things into perspective, in our childhood and adolescence. Heightened emotional experiences, such as fear, are even more challenging for our young brains. When our parents divorce, our grandparents die, or we experience failure or humiliation, our brains quickly acquire values that will prevent us from experiencing the same trauma again. Even stuff that seems harmless to adults can leave long-lasting marks on the psyche of kids.

Experts call these emotionally charged events *small social traumas*. By the time we're seventeen, our brains are mature enough to handle the scary stuff. But seventeen years is a long time, especially when we're in the thick of those years. Plenty of time to rack up our fair share of public humiliations, traumatic changes, and frightening situations. Here are some striking, yet real-life examples.

"IN LIFE, SOMEONE HAS TO EAT SH*T"

What is the first thing you remember about self-reliance?

During a coaching session, Marie identified *self-reliance* as an acquired value. She recalled a fight between her parents when she was a child. She remembers the loud voices that frightened her, but she also vividly remembers how upset she felt when her father stormed out of the house and didn't return. Her mom, tired and tearful, lit a cigarette and slumped in her chair.

"In life, someone has to eat sh*t," her mom said. "And it's always the woman."

Marie's young brain wasn't able to put any of this into a useful perspective. Instead, she learned that as a woman, she should expect to be treated poorly. The only way to avoid a fate like her mom's? Never let anyone get close enough to disrespect you; never rely on anyone but yourself.

Twenty-five years later, Marie's frantic need to feel independent shapes her work life and relationships. A career achiever, Marie progressed from an internship to a top position in her company in only two years. She's now earning a PhD from a well-known university, and she commands respect as her colleagues recognize her dedication and fairness. Meanwhile, her intimate relationships have suffered from her lack of ability to compromise or be vulnerable. She says she wants a serious and committed relationship, but when things get serious and she finds herself opening up emotionally, she self-sabotages relationship after relationship. She believes if she depended on *anyone*, she'd be the one who'd end up eating poo.

Marie mixed up a harmful dependency on boyfriends (when she'd *need* them to function) with "interdependence," (where she'd feel *safe* to rely on each other in healthy ways). She's attracted to men who want fun and light relationships, only to eventually blame them for enjoying life on their separate budgets. And those who were committed and obviously wanted to settle? Booooring. Without a healthy, mature voice to help Marie-the-Child understand that her mother's experiences don't necessarily have to be hers, Marie-the-Adult sacrifices true intimacy to preserve her self-respect and self-sufficiency at all costs.

"You Stupid Cow!"

Corina easily traces her desire for *knowledge* to an art class when she was only eight years old. Excited by some new colors of paint her teacher offered the students, Corina immediately began dabbing her brush into one that shimmered like gold. She played with brushstrokes on the paper, dipping her brush in the gold, again and again, delighted by the sheen.

As the teacher walked behind the students, studying their progress, she stopped when she got to Corina. Expecting praise for her shiny masterpiece, Corina was stunned when, instead, her teacher screamed, "You stupid cow!"

In front of the whole class, her teacher went on to reprimand her for not paying attention . . . for not listening when she was instructed to use the gold sparingly, for highlights alone . . . for not understanding how expensive it was . . . Corina wanted to crawl under her desk and cry.

The social context of the classroom added to the trauma. Corina's art class took place in Switzerland where it is extremely insulting and rare to call someone a *stupid cow*. You just don't do that. Ever. Eventually, the teacher apologized to Corina, but it was too late. The incident scarred her deeply. Her sense of curiosity and play immediately transformed into a sense of shame.

Corina needed someone to help her understand that her teacher's outburst was not really about her. The teacher took her own stress about some problem of her own out on Corina and Corina's eight-year-old brain wasn't mature enough to contextualize and understand other perspectives. Instead, she blamed herself for being so stupid, and this social trauma burned deep into her psyche.

Ever since, Corina has been proving to herself and the world that she's not a stupid cow. Secretly, she was afraid she'd someday be revealed for the "stupid" imposter she believed, deep down, she was. She *had* to know *everything*. An excellent student, she now enjoys a career as an academic project manager. In order to follow the scientific conversations of her researcher coworkers, she spent hours Googling topics she didn't understand, like the excretory system of worms. Her quest for knowledge came from a place of fear rather than from true curiosity, and her self-confidence, at work and elsewhere, suffered.

Thanks to her values coaching, Corina now recognizes when she's blaming herself for not knowing as much as others. Now, when a co-worker boasts about his latest discoveries during coffee breaks, Corina doesn't feel anxious for not keeping up. She listens politely, secretly wondering what *his* acquired values must be. What must his own childhood have been like, if today, he's such a show-off at work?

Corina and Marie's stories are real, as well as extreme, and carefully selected to help you understand the power of unchecked acquired values. Not all of our acquired values show up so dramatically. Their effects can be subtle and nuanced. With awareness, you'll see how values you adopted in your past may be tripping you up today.

WHY YOU GOTTA' BRING UP OLD SH*T?

By now, you're well past Psych 101, and you're ready to move on to blaming your parents for all your misery, fully armed with science and fancy words to back you up. Just kidding. Well, sort of. You are certainly past Psych 101 if you've made it to Chapter 5. And you are definitely ready to take a long, hard look at your circle of immediate influencers and consider how they've shaped the person you are today.

So, who makes up that inner circle of immediate influencers? Who has VIP access to *you*?

Once you've sketched out who your immediate influencers are, it's time to take a look at any possible beliefs or behaviors you may have picked up from those closest to you.

Ooof. Not all of us are always eager to revisit our upbringing. You may be asking, *who wants to rehash the past and re-live unpleasant, perhaps even traumatic memories*? If you think now that dragging the stuff from past out into the light is the last thing you want to do, I totally understand. I've been there, too. If you are like my friend, Charlie, who enjoyed a happy childhood with delightful, loving, and self-aware parents, and you have nothing but happy memories . . . well, you're probably not reading this book.

For the rest of us, here's what I can share: The more resistant you are to exploring your family of origin, the more likely you need to. The more you distract yourself with computer games, red wine, social media, shopping, or Netflix, the more likely you'll benefit from asking provocative questions about your life.

I should warn you, though, that digging deep into your past isn't a ten-minute reflection exercise. It's hard and scary to re-wire our adult brains. It's especially difficult to face the fears we've nurtured or neglected since our childhood or adolescence. But the monster under the bed will only get larger and creepier until you turn on the lights and see for yourself that the only things under your bed are several missing socks, some hairbands, and dust bunnies. Similarly, once you connect your inner demons to the exact situations in which those demons were born, their voices will gradually become quieter and quieter. Finally, when they become almost noiseless, you'll be free to follow only those values that truly serve you. You'll be the one to decide what *being you* is all about.

And one last little remark: While our focus has been on the troublesome and even traumatic stuff we've acquired from our parents, let's be clear—not everything our parents told us is crap. You may find some advice useful, some values worthwhile. It's up to *you*, with your awareness and discernment, to decide what serves you and what doesn't.

Thought Experiment: So, Tell Me about Your Mother . . .

Grab that glass of single-malt or wine, and let's get into it.

- What moments (and parental advice) from your childhood and adolescence have stuck with you the most?
- Think about how your family describes themselves. For example, "The Hernandez family is always hospitable" or "The Mabes always persevere, no matter what."
- Which of your accomplishments did your parents "brag" about?
- Using the values list in the Appendix, identify the values behind those stories. How have you been shaped by these values?

Chapter 6

Generational Values

When I was younger, I scorned everything "trendy" or "cool." I felt miles (or kilometers) away from my peers, a loveable misfit. A friend of mine recalls how, as a teenager, there was nothing worse than anything "mainstream." It's funny how so many of us take pride in being different from the herd. No matter how at odds with the world we may feel, the truth is that all of us truly do internalize the strong influences of our generation. Those values prized by society at specific points in time become our acquired values, the result of our circumstances and the fads of our peers.

As you read this chapter, you may—and I hope you do—recognize some of yourself in the values of your generation. But, more than that, my intention in this chapter is to offer you a window into *other* generational values. Understanding the differences between your acquired generational values and someone else's helps you better understand *yourself*. Importantly, generational self-awareness is a surefire way to help you spot those moments when you might be acting (just a teeny tiny bit, of course) judgmental. When you have a better understanding of where your acquired values might clash with your grandparent or grandchild, boss or employee, teacher or student, or the annoying person in the supermarket, the better your chances are for fostering wellbeing and healthy relationships.

At the end of the day, all of us, regardless of our age, share the same ultimate goal: to fulfill our three basic psychological needs of autonomy, competence, and connection. But how we go about it can be wildly different. The way we pursue our goals evolves over time—and that's mostly why generations clash.

AH, KIDS TODAY

Popular discourse around the millennial generation gives us the impression that millennials are the first generation to be wildly different from older generations.[30] And yet, ancient Greek philosophers, Socrates and Plato, critiqued the youngsters for their love of luxury, disrespect of authority, bad manners, and oppressing their teachers.[31]

Plato's remarks suggest that, at least since 428 B.C.E., humans have been experiencing "generation gaps," which usually goes something like this:

Older: "Back in *my* day…" or "Kids these days don't have any respect for [fill in the blank]."

Younger: "You just don't get it." or "Times have changed, Dad."

On one hand, there is a tendency of older generations to fail to cherish evolving youth cultures and values. On the other, younger generations insist the older generations are "stuck in the past" and out of touch with the world. To understand why this gap exists and put our acquired values into perspective, let's look at why and how generations differ from one another.

CRACKING THE GENERATIONAL CODE

To deeply understand generations of people and what makes them tick, it's useful to remember these groups are usually categorized by events rather than arbitrary dates. Keep in mind that the concept of "generations" is a construct. While research attaches certain characteristics to certain periods of time, these ideas are not set in stone. Rather, generations exist on a continuum—and there is a large degree of individual variation within them.

In the United States, for example, how generational values play out varies as a result of social difference. The legal segregation of African-Americans, which lasted until 1964, made it much harder for Blacks to pursue and achieve

30   Caraher, Lee. *Millennials & Management: The Essential Guide To Making It Work At Work.* Brookline, MA: Bibliomotion, 2014.
31   Attributed to Socrates by Plato, according to William L. Patty, Louise S. Johnson. *Personality and Adjustment.* New York: McGraw-Hill, 1953.

the "American Dream" that formed a cornerstone of traditional mid-century American values. Other ethnic and minority groups also faced socio-economic challenges that influenced how, and to what extent, individuals acquired generational values. As you read the following sections, keep in mind these generational characteristics are general and may not apply to all. In fact, it might be a valuable thought experiment to ask yourself how social differences may have influenced the pursuit of each generation's set of acquired values. Finally, remember the generation to which we belong is only one of several factors that influence how we see the world (i.e. our value system).

Every generation has been shaped by the world as they came of age. Three key factors impact generational values: major global and national events, popular culture, and family dynamics. Let's take a look at the impact these three factors have had on five recent generational groupings: **civic/silent generation** (born 1925–1945); **baby boomers** (born 1946–1964); **Generation X** (born 1965–1980) **millennials** (born 1981–1995); and **Generation Z** (born 1996–2009).

As you read about the experiences of each generation, consider how different their world was from the world you were born into. Ask yourself: *If I were born at a different time, would I share that generation's values and survival instincts?*

Civic/Silent Generation (Born 1925–1945)

Context: The Dream Postponed

Silents were raised by parents who fought to survive the Great Depression, working multiple jobs to make ends meet. As a result, they played it safe, avoided risk, and kept their heads down. Eager to help their country re-build from the chaos of world wars, they believed they could make a difference through hard work and determination. As a result, *Time Magazine* labeled them "Silent" in a famous 1951 essay.[32]

Because the hard work of the silent generation dragged the USA out of The Depression and into prosperity, they valued and pursued wealth creation and stability. By achieving "the American Dream," silents were acting on their

---

32   "People: The Younger Generation." *Time Magazine*, 1951, accessed 10 Feb 2021, http://content.time.com/time/subscriber/article/0,33009,856950,00.html.

generational values, manufacturing a suburban world where they and their children could, for the first time in their lives, feel safe. As some silents prospered and others suffered from Jim Crow laws and segregation, racial disparities became starker and clearer, fueling the subsequent generation's embrace of values such as justice and equality.

Culture: "It Don't Mean a Thing (If It Ain't Got That Swing)"[33]

Caught up in the Great Depression and its immediate aftermath, and with the world's focus on World War II, having fun, belonging, and relaxation were all rooted in wartime conditions and overcoming obstacles. Silents expressed the values of their generation through their rich musical traditions. Through jazz and the Blues, musicians like Cab Calloway, Duke Ellington, Count Basie, Ella Fitzgerald, and Billie Holiday could give voice to the frustrated dreams of African-Americans on the one hand and celebrate a raucous enjoyment of life on the other. In doing so, jazz and the Blues captured the tension between this generation's longing for *stability* and their need to let loose and forget about war, unemployment, hunger, and social inequity. Jazz offshoots Swing and Big Band were more watered-down, mainstream versions of jazz, where (white, middle-class) young people could forget their wartime woes and dance it out to Cole Porter or Frank Sinatra. The end of this generation saw the birth of rock n' roll, whose powerful alchemy transformed the world-weariness of the Blues and wildness of jazz into a celebration of teenage culture and defiance, heralding the arrival of a new generation and a shift in generational values from *security* and *survival* to *questioning* and *freedom*.

Family Dynamics: Children Should be Seen but Not Heard

One of the most elegant ways to follow the family dynamics of a generation is to compare the different books on childrearing. The style of parenting known to the silents and the generations before them originated in the late 1800s. In 1928, the best-selling parenting guide was *Psychological Care of Infant and Child* by John Watson. As Chair of Psychology at Johns Hopkins University, Watson

---

33   Duke Ellington (lyrics written by Irving Mills), "It Don't Mean a Thing (If It Ain't Got That Swing)." Studio recording, 1931.

believed children shouldn't cry "unless stuck by a pin." Watson's main message for moms was that their love was dangerous. If a child exhibited any troubling behavior, it was the mother's fault. He writes, "Mothers just don't know, when they kiss their children and pick them up and rock them, caress them and jiggle them upon their knee, that they are slowly building up a human being totally unable to cope with the world it must later live in." Then he elaborated on how to fix what's broken: "Never hug and kiss them. Never let them sit on your lap. If you must, kiss them once on the forehead when they say good night. Shake hands with them in the morning."[34]

Today we have visceral reactions to the emotional detachment Watson promotes, and we question how in the world moms and dads back then could actually raise their children in this way. On the surface, at least, it seems we're wildly different from families who lived one hundred years ago.

Let's go a bit deeper, though. Surely, parents in the 1920s loved their kids as much as we love our children today. Let's remember that there were few sources describing how to raise your kids (and although Watson has ample detractors, he does deserve credit for launching child development as a field of study). New parents had no support groups and "google" was not yet a verb. People needed information, and they respected Johns Hopkins University and Watson's book as *the authority*. Imagine how hard it would have been to say, *I know better, even though I'm not a psychologist*. If their children did struggle in life, the parents likely blamed themselves for not following Watson's manual with enough care.

If you wonder how Watson's theories resonated with higher institutions in the first place, don't forget that in the circles of prominent psychologists of the time, it was widely accepted that without controlling them, "humans were homicidal barbarians." And churches or organizations "representing" faith and religion were not helping either.

As a parent, I've asked myself, *would I be influenced by Watson's advice if I had had my little ones at those times?* Wow. Chances are I would have. I'm a reader, and I love understanding human nature. I likely would have read his manual, and I'd have felt horribly insulted as a woman. Yet a shadow of guilt would fall over me every time I'd (excessively) kiss my kids.

---

34   Watson, John B. *Psychological Care of Infant and Child.* New York City: W.W. Norton & Co, 1928.

Family Dynamics: We Don't Raise Tyrants in Europe . . . Er . . .

Up until now, we've focused our discussion mainly on the United States. But the situation in Europe was not that much different. Across the continent, nations were steeped in a culture that valued duty and control, and popular books on parents reflected a remarkable toughness in child rearing. In the 1930s, a pulmonologist with no pediatric training, Johanna Haarer, published two parenting manuals. Her first book, *The German Mother and Her First Child*, sold a whooping 1.2 million copies. Like Watson, she argued that parents needed to break the will of their baby or risk him becoming an "implacable house tyrant" (apparently there was only room for one tyrant, and we all know who was busy with the job). Haarer also instructed moms to leave their babies alone except for feeding and bathing, to have little physical contact even when carrying them, and to ignore them when they cry—especially at bedtime.[35]

Generational Values: A Penny Saved is a Penny Earned

Silents understood the need to delay their personal dream for the greater good. They valued dedication and sacrifice and understood grit and determination in a way no generation has since. The traditionalists came of age at a time when they trusted their government and respected authority (I recall my grandma fighting with my mom, saying, "How can you say it's a lie; it has just been aired on the TV?"). They are loyal, and they desire respect and honesty in return.

While there are always exceptions, silents generally strove for and embodied respect, dignity, discipline, responsibilities, manners, dedication, sacrifice, hard work, conformity, loyalty, stability, security, authority, delayed reward, patience, duty, saving, and tradition. If you want to understand a civic/silent, ask them what the most creative thing they ever did with their wartime rations was.

A Note on Geography

Although no two countries or regions share exactly the same values (see Chapter 7), from the post-war period on, new developments in technology, such as the television and, later, the Internet, helped create a *general* set of shared

---

35   Haarer, Johanna. *Die deutsche Mutter und ihr erstes Kind*, Berlin: Lehmanns, München, 1934.

generational values for young people around the world, particularly in North America and Europe. So while the application of these generational values might look different in different places, from here on out, we'll focus on those shared values that came to define subsequent generations on both sides of the pond.

Baby Boomers (Born 1946–1964)

Context: "The Times They Are A-Changin'"[36]

With World War II behind them and a robust American economy, silents/civics finally lived in a relatively stable world. And so they had babies. Lots of them. Hence this new generation's name—the baby boomers. In the early boomer era, many silent generation parents wanted to give their children everything they didn't have when they were young. Boomers learned from their parents' post-war prosperity that they could be, have, and do anything.

Yet, once again, the world around them was changing rapidly. Social unrest and scientific and technological advancements infused boomers with a sense of limitless possibilities that translated into the values of *optimism*, *hard work*, and a "yes, we can" spirit. As teenagers, boomers rebelled against the rigidity of their parents' worldview, giving rise to a youth culture that valued *freedom* and *personal expression*. The "hippies" and "radicals" grew their hair long, smoked marijuana, practiced "free love," and sincerely believed they could change the world. The idealism and activism of the boomers helped fuel the Civil Rights Movement and the fight for gender equality. There was the Space Race, the moon landing, air travel—all proof to boomers they could have/do/be anything.

As boomers left college and became part of the workforce, they began to value work and professional success. Raised with the promise that if you succeed financially you'll be happy, many put their careers before their families and came to see themselves primarily as workers, finding value in professional status. Boomers brought us the sixty-hour work week (thanks, boomer) and the "so, what do you do?" conversation starter. They also expected their employees

36 Bob Dylan, "The Times They Are a-Chagin'" The Times They Are a-Changin' Studio Album. Columbia Records, 1964.

to share their work ethic and be as committed to and invested in their jobs. Remember Nina from the Introduction?

Culture: "What's Going On"[37]

We are still fascinated with boomer pop culture. Crafted from the crucible of radical social change and fierce convictions, boomer pop culture of the 1960s and 1970s expressed and reinforced the generation's values. Boomers are the rock n' roll and disco generation, genres that provided the soundtracks to values of *rebellion, change,* and *hedonism.* For *young* boomer, "cool" meant rebellion against the strict rules and conservative attitudes of their parents. Cool meant jeans and no bras, to kiss boys *and* girls, and to try drugs. At every live concert, march for Civil Rights, and anti-war protest, they relished the electricity in the air. They experienced an incredible sense of possibility.

As boomers grew up, they channeled their energy and enthusiasm into their work. By the 1980s, boomers had morphed from radicals to yuppies. Now "cool" was to be busy, make lots of money, spend it conspicuously, own the largest house and car your money could buy, have parquet floors and a maid, and to take expensive vacations. Mostly confident that they'd solved the United States' social problems, boomers valued the individual over the collective. *You* have to gain material wealth and possessions for *your* family. Not community, not society, not greater good, but *you. You*'re doing well if *you* have the title and the house with a pool because *you* deserve it. Appearance, once rejected by their teenage selves, became more important. Women aerobicized and men jogged their way to perfect bodies. And, yes, there was that whole thing with Spandex, shoulder pads, and keyboard neckties.

Family Dynamics: "Papa Don't Preach"[38]

In 1946, Dr. Benjamin Spock's book,[39] *The Common Sense Book of Baby and Child Care*, transformed parenting. Among *Time*'s Top 100 Books of

---

37   Marvin Gaye. "What's Going On." *What's Going On.* Self-produced, 1971.
38   Brian Elliot and Madonna. "Papa Don't Preach." *The Immaculate Collection.* Warner Records, 1986.
39   Spock, Benjamin. *The Common Sense Book of Baby and Child Care.* New York: Duell, Sloan and Pearce, 1946.

All-Time (it topped best-seller lists for over sixty-five years), this book sold nine million copies to parents seeking additional help and support in raising children between its publishing date of 1946 and 1957. By the time Dr. Spock died in 1998, his book had sold fifty million copies. So, what made his advice so popular?

Imagine being a woman who, for years, had been told that her love was dangerous to her child. Now she learns that it's her love that makes her child whole! Dr. Spock told parents that the more scientists and clinicians explored different approaches to parenting, the more they were convinced that intuitive decisions mothers and fathers made served their babies best. Dr. Spock, a pediatrician, emphasized above all that parents should feel confident and trust their instincts. "Trust yourself." With these first words, Spock revolutionized child-rearing methods and shifted the generational values for the post-World War II generations.

Spock's manual indicated a major cultural shift in the ways American society viewed parents' roles in raising children. This shift let "kids be kids" and encouraged parents to let the natural progression of childhood to adulthood ensue, something the silent generation did not receive from their parents.

Generational Values: Work Hard, Play Hard

The post-war prosperity, their parents' conviction that hard work really pays off, and a parenting style that encourages individualism and less restriction all contributed to the shift from discipline and conformity to feeling entitled to take over the world if you work hard enough. Baby boomers came of age as the United States and Western countries became superpowers, so they're an optimistic bunch, believing no challenge is too great.

Baby boomers are more educated than previous generations, and they're known for working hard and playing hard. Not surprisingly, they measure success by what they own and value glory, prestige, recognition, fame, social status, power, money, workaholism, position, materialism, competition, individualism, independence, achievement, non-conformity, and legacy. If you really want to get to know a boomer, ask them what "See the USA in your Chevrolet" means.

Generation X (Born 1965–1980)

Context: Reality Bites

In a 2017 article for *Vanity Fair*, Rich Cohen described Gen X as squeezed between two vast generations, boomers and millennials: "[…] the last Americans schooled in the old manner, the last Americans that know how to fold a newspaper, take a joke, and listen to a dirty story without losing their minds."[40] The memory of a childhood spent outdoors, and the analogue world dies with this generation. For Gen X, the disillusionment continues.

In contrast to other generations, commonly described by what they believe, Xers are mostly known for what they *don't* believe. They largely rejected their parents' beliefs, receiving the "X" tag for lack of a defining social identity. Gen Xers, who came of age in a post-Vietnam War and post-Cold War era, were raised with the promises of equal opportunity and American global dominance. Yet the events of the '80s and '90s largely betrayed everything Gen Xers had been told.

This generation navigated a world shaped by the Watergate scandal and President Nixon's resignation, surging oil process and gas shortages, nuclear power disasters (Chernobyl), the violent death of the Space Program when the Space Shuttle Challenger exploded on live TV, the Iran-Contra affair, and the first war in Iraq. Boomers called Gen Xers apathetic, disillusioned, aimless, and cynical—values they themselves often embraced as they watched politicians lie, their parents get laid off, and the whole apparatus of the "American Dream" dismantle before their eyes. Because they've seen and heard so many lies growing up, GenXers value *honesty* more than any other generation.

As the economy vacillated between lows and highs throughout the '70s and '80s, Gen Xers got the message that hard work did not necessarily equal stability, let alone happiness. They are first generation that will not do as well financially as their parents. They have lower financial net worth than previous groups had at this same age, and they lost nearly half of their wealth in the Great Recession

---

40   Cohen, Rich. "Why Generation X Might Be Our Last, Best Hope." *Vanity Fair*, 2017, accessed 10 Feb 2021, https://www.vanityfair.com/style/2017/08/why-generation-x-might-be-our-last-best-hope.

of 2008.[41] Neither totally destitute, like their grandparents' childhoods, nor wealth-obsessed, like their parents, Gen Xers have seen it all and respond with detachment, irony, and a weariness toward history. They are impatient with both brands of utopianism (boomer and millennial). Profoundly misunderstood (adding fuel to the Gen X fire of cynical wariness) as "slackers," Gen Xer's are not aimless and unmotivated, just the unlucky-but-inevitable inheritors of a derelict dream.

However, Gen Xers have made the best of being the "middle child." The first generation to have computers in their childhood homes and the first generation not confused by email, they quickly turned their ability to adapt to new technology into troubleshooting and problem-solving skills. Gen Xers have avoided the workaholism of their parents by demanding a better work-life balance but have the strongest work ethic among current generations. Go figure.

Culture: "Smells Like Teen Spirit"[42]

As adolescents and young adults in the 1980s and 1990s, Xers were dubbed the "MTV Generation" because the emergence of music videos defined pop culture during their teen years. In the '80s, pop rock stars like Madonna and Michael Jackson appealed to Gen Xers' appreciation of fun and inclusivity, while the emerging hip hop genre rapped about *individuality, self-reliance,* and *freedom.* In the early '90s, no band was more iconic than Nirvana, no tragic anti-hero more apathetic than Kurt Cobain. Cobain spoke for the skeptic, down-to-earth, dirty-haired, flannel-wearing, coffee-soaked disaffected youth. His suicide in 1994 was interpreted by boomers as proof of apathy's dangerous moral corruption. To young Gen Xers, however, the tragedy became a symbol of society's failure to care, fueling their cynical disillusionment. Yet, as adults, Gen Xers have largely re-framed Cobain's death as proof of why freedom and fun must be balanced with hard work and honesty—with yourself and with others. Cobain's lyrics in the ironically-titled "Smells Like Teen Spirit" (a generational

---

41   "Retirement Security Across Generations: Are Americans Prepared for Their Golden Years." *Pew Charitable Trust,* 2013, accessed 10 Feb 2021, https://www.pewtrusts.org/en/research-and-analysis/reports/0001/01/01/retirement-security-across-generations.

42   Nirvana. "Smells Like Teen Spirit." *Nevermind. DGC Records,* 1991.

anthem to some) distilled the MTV generation thusly: a working generation wanting to be "entertained."

Family Dynamics: Latchkey Kids

Although Spock's manual was still ruling the world of parenting, Gen Xers were children during a time when society moved from a 1950s-era "cult of the child" to a 1970s-era "cult of the adult." The long-held societal value of staying together for the sake of the children was slowly giving way to parental and individual self-actualization, which changed traditional family structures. More women were rejecting having to choose between staying at home to parent or entering the workforce. No longer staying together "for the sake of the children," a growing number of couples divorced. Divorce rates doubled in the mid-1960s before peaking in 1980.

Childcare options for working parents were limited as society adjusted to re-structured families. As a result, Gen Xers were the first generation of children to return to an empty home after school or left at home without supervision because their parent(s) were away at work, thus earning them the label "latchkey kids." Though many of Gen Xers are children of "broken homes," their unhappy experiences have provoked a determination to provide the opposite for their own offspring. As parents, Gen Xers value *flexibility, responsibility,* and *balance.*

Generational Values: A Tribe Called Quest

Fiercely independent, Gen Xers had to figure things out for themselves and carve out their own paths, somewhere between the overbearing boomers and self-righteous indignation of millennials. Gen Xers are less likely to value material possessions for the sake of appearances; they don't drive an SUV as a symbol of masculinity but because it makes sense when you have three kids, a stroller, and seven sets of reserve outfits as a regular accessory. They still wear flannels but have a college savings account for their kids. In general, they value: honesty, inclusion, balance, diversity, fun, flexibility, individuality, freedom, responsibility, pragmatism, informality, self-reliance, skepticism, and down-to-earthness. If you want to know more about the values of a Gen Xer, ask him or her (they're not yet used to gender neutral pronouns) to tell you about his/her favorite mix tape.

Millennials (Born 1981–1995)

Context: All About (Social) ME(dia)

With the approaching new millennium, the millennial generation was born into a fast-paced world of advancing technology and large cultural shifts. While Gen X was techno-savvy, the millennials are techno-fused, and their identity and corresponding values are closely tied to the birth of modern digital media. In their childhood and teenage years, millennials witnessed many immense and defining problems of modern society, including 9/11, school shootings, the AIDS epidemic, and on-going wars in the Middle East. Yet their parents worked hard to shelter their millennial children from the world's harsh realities. Their children received trophies not for winning but simply for participating. They grew up with lessons on "self-esteem" in school and were encouraged to follow their dreams. For these reasons, millennials have been stereotyped as "coddled kids."

Millennials recognized early on that advice from their parents wasn't going to work in their brave, new world. For previous generations, post-secondary education was broadly financially remunerative, but Generation X marked the last generation in the United States for whom this was the case. For millennials and Gen Z, education beyond high school did not necessarily equate to a lucrative or stable career. Millennials started questioning the system their parents created, and they joined social justice classes and clubs *en masse* in high school. As a result of increased social awareness at early ages, many millennials turned to community service and activism to help combat these problems.

As children growing up with digital media, millennials had more unprecedented access to information than previous generations. Their access to all this information led to fear of missing out (FOMO) in their social lives. Prioritizing is not easy for them because they don't want to miss out on anything and so try instead to do everything. Millennials are well informed, aware of challenges, socially conscious, and want to help fix things for the greater good.

They crave clear ways to measure their progress, as the perceived road to success has been mapped out for them their entire lives by their parents. This civic-minded and engaged generation has big hopes for the future, yet they lack the grit and resilience of silents, the grassroots organizing abilities of the boomers, and the work ethic of Gen Xers.

Culture: Through the #Blessed Filter

To millennials, popular culture *is* the Internet and social media. Millennials live and display their lives on Facebook, Instagram, Twitter, TikTok, YouTube, Tumblr, Reddit, and other social media websites and have introduced hundreds of new words into our everyday lexicon. Before this generation, verbs like "vlogging," "Facebooking," "trolling," "force quitting" or nouns such as "meme" or "selfie" did not exist. Millennials send 2,700 texts per month on average, have popularized social media stars, created careers, such as Youtubers or Instagram Influencers, and are expected to take 25,700 selfies in their lifetime.[43] Rejecting the Gen X mantra that "reality bites," millennials have re-defined reality altogether by blurring the boundaries between "real" life and their social media personas.

Extensive and mostly unsupervised use of the Internet contributed to the obsession of young generations with being rich and famous. Young millennials watched rags-to-riches success stories through their favorite reality TV shows and social media sites on a daily basis. News feeds provide a continuous reel of young billionaires, athletes, and celebrities with #amazing lifestyles representing ultimate achievement and happiness. Alongside increased awareness around issues such as inequality, millennials place high value on *status, money, wealth, fame, rewards, reputation* or *admiration* (I mean, "Get Rich or Die Tryin'"[44], right?). No, the contradiction doesn't bother them. #YOLO

Whatever fears and security threats existed irl, millennials could pursue their values online. Culture and social life began to take place in chat rooms, message boards, Facebook, and online dating sites, offering millennials a safer space to pursue community, connection, acceptance, and fun. As online dating moved from the dubious, uncool fringes of the digital world to full-on mainstream, it

---

43   Glum, Julia. "Millennials Selfies: Young Adults Will Take More Than 25,000 Pictures Of Themselves During Their Lifetimes: Report." *International Business Times*, 2015.

44   50 Cent. "Get Rich or Die Tryin'. *50 Cent. Shady Records*, 2003.

fundamentally changed even the most intimate experiences of our lives. Boomers met their partners in college, Gen Xers met in bars or underground shows, but millennials "hooked up" via algorithms, "d*ck pics," "sexy selfies," and having their smartphone's location services on at the right place at the right time. Good-bye cheesy pick-up lines in bars, and hello "wyd" texts.

Family Dynamics: "You're Hovering, Mom!"

Millennial babies were literally given all the opportunities the world has to offer but with one little caveat: their parents tried to protect them from everything scary or unfair coming along the way—their parents sort of vowed to relentlessly protect their babies from the "evils" of the world.

In a series of interviews published in *Millennials Rising*,[45] a book written in 2000 by Howe and Strauss, parents reported they could still recall and "feel" the shift in parents' attitude in the early '80s. In her dissertation from the University of Colorado, Lauren Troksa linked the beginning of the era of the over-protected children to a horrifying event from September 1982, when small amounts of cyanide were detected in the Halloween treats given to young kids.[46]

From the boomer perspective, protective and engaged parenting made sense. Boomers who grew up with a prosperous economy were now raising kids in and around the repercussions of a failing economy. These "material girls and guys" feared their children might make "wrong" academic or career decisions and end up overeducated and underemployed. A new, overprotective way of parenting emerged, commonly known as *helicopter parenting*. Helicopter parenting refers to when a parent hovers over their child like a helicopter, rescuing him or her at the first sign of danger or lack of happiness. Parents made sure to "helicopter" over their children early enough because they perceived straight *As* from preschool on as a ticket for enrolling the college that will enable the shiny future. Also, to make sure they did everything on their end for creating "well-rounded" college applicants, parents persuaded children into busy schedules of sports, hobbies, and other interests. By the late 1980s, over 70 percent of children participated

45   Howe, Neil and William Strauss. *Millennials Rising*. New York: Vintage Books, 2000.
46   Troksa, Lauren. "The Study of Generations: A Timeless Notion within a Contemporary Context." Dissertation, Department of History at the University of Colorado Boulder, 2016.

in extracurricular activities.[47] Indeed, Reyne Rice, from the Toy Industry Association in New York, shared her observations that parents of millennials see their children's education as a top priority, and they are willing to invest whatever resources are needed to give their kids a pole position in the race of life.[48]

Generational Values: Back to the Future

Millennials embody a tug of war between their own desires and the overprotective influence of their parents, creating a dichotomy of values and traits. They are optimistic but anxious, goal-orientated but indecisive, and competitive but poor at handling losses. In the age of social media, they value appearances and material possessions but are also more accepting of others' differences. In part due to the influence of their boomer parents, millennials value achievement, admiration, fame, reward, confidence, ambition, competition, and fun. From their own ability to research information within seconds and an increased awareness as they mature, millennials also emphasize and embody civic duty, family, open-mindedness, acceptance, and spirituality. If you really want to get to know a millennial, ask them about their first Tinder date.

Generation Z (Born 1996–2009)

Context: Woke Warriors

If you were born in 1996 or later, you don't remember 9/11. You cannot process the world as it was before the attacks—or the world before the Internet. You are a part of Generation Z, also known as the iGen. Born mainly to Gen Xers, but also to millennials, the eldest of this generation are perhaps the last to have been born in an optimistic world that seemed to be on a more stable trajectory. Most, however, were born into a world rocked by new levels of global terrorism, climate change, financial instability/The Great Recession, school shootings and gun violence, mass incarceration rates in the USA, and populist backlash that often touted extreme forms of nationalism and xenophobia.

---

47   Wong, Alia. "The Activity Gap." *The Atlantic*, 2015, accessed 10 Feb, 20201, https://www. theatlantic.com/education/archive/2015/01/the-activity-gap/384961/.

48   Wall, Barbara. "Ambitious Parents Spend on Educational Toys for Toddlers." *International Herald Tribune*. New York Times, 2006.

Influenced by such world events and major socio-economic paradigm shifts, Gen Zers are conscientious, hardworking, somewhat anxious, and mindful of the future. Jason Dorsey at the Center of Generational Kinetics has observed that like their parents from Generation X, members of Generation Z tend to be autonomous and pessimistic—leaving the optimism behind while embracing pragmatism.

Born to Gen Z parents, they inherited their thick skin and the ability to endure rough environment. While "feeling under-appreciated" is a strong reason for 25 percent of millennials to leave their current job, a huge majority of Gen Z rather sees their jobs as means to an end and doesn't need the affirmation sought by their older peers.[49] Gen Z share with boomers the dubious privilege of watching their parents bear the brunt of recession. As a result, they typically become financially literate at an earlier age, and their longing for financial security is by far outweighing their desire for ownership, giving rise to sharing-economy.[50]

Exposed to more of the world at earlier ages thanks to social media, Gen Z values diversity. Unlike Gen Xers and millennials, who came of age alongside the Internet, Generation Z represent the first true digital natives. They might have had Facebook pages, created by their parents, before they could talk or walk. In general, they don't focus as much on social difference as some of our older counterparts might. A Black man occupied the White House for a significant portion of their lives, and gay marriage was old news by the time they were born. But they are not colorblind, pretending to a fake equality—indeed, Gen Zers are generally more attuned to all forms of social privilege, i.e. "woke". Gen Zers apprehend and recognize social injustice; they just don't quite get why can't we already solve it.

Culture: A New Kind of Buzzy

In their social behavior and cultural traits, Gen Z values *security, independence, progress, entrepreneurship, privacy, leadership, learning,* and *creativity.* They're

---

49 The Deloitte Global Millennial Survey 2019: "Societal Discord and Technological Transformation Create a 'Generation disrupted.'" *Deloitte,* 2019.

50 Boyle, Matthew and Matthew Townsend. "Reality Bites Back: To understand Gen Z, Look To the Gen X Parents." *Bloomberg,* 2019.

a more conservative bunch, even resembling silents in some ways. Bryan Gildenberg, the chief knowledge officer at Kantar Consulting, refers to Gen Zers as a "very old group of young people" that practices behaviors that are the opposite of what we expect from youngsters: less sex, drugs (a remark here is they consider pot a medicine) and rock 'n' roll.[51] Sorry boomers, not even your young selves would be cool for this generation.

Unlike typical teenagers of other generations, Generation Z members worry more about big problems, such as their future, than about dating or gangs. Coolness and belonging are taking shape around eco-movements—heaven forbid you use a plastic straw when hanging with a Gen Zer (and rightfully so). With all the (literally) burning problems of the world, finally there is a generation that has to take fighting climate change seriously. For this generation, being an eco-warrior is much cooler than rebelling against parents or studying for the SAT exam.

Although they keep their expectations limited, members of this generation will put everything on the line to win. Entertaining, but at the same time challenging, reality shows have inspired them to embrace entrepreneurship while, in parallel, they've witnessed how leveraging technology can create exciting and profitable businesses with low starting investment.[52] Fifty-eight percent of Gen Zers contemplate running their own business, while 14 percent of them already do, as reported by XYZ University in 2018.[53]

Family Dynamics: You Got This

Corey Seemiller, a professor at Ohio's Wright State University who's been studying Gen Zers for years, argues that the parenting goal of Gen X is to raise Gen Z to resemble their own "phenotype" very much—to be self-directed, skeptical, and flexible to adjust to a speedily-changing world. Gen X parents encourage their Gen Z kids to figure things out for themselves and don't helicopter. Instead, Gen Xers are "stealth fighter parents," letting minor issues go

---

51 Boyle, Matthew and Matthew Townsend. "Reality Bites Back: To understand Gen Z, Look To the Gen X Parents."

52 Miller, Josh. "A 16-Year-Old Explains 10 Things You Need to Know About Generation Z," *Society for Human Resource Management (SHRM)*, 2018.

53 "Ready or Not—Here Comes Z," *XYZ University*, 2018.

and refusing to micromanage their kids' education but intervening forcefully and swiftly in the event of more serious issues.[54] Gen Zers grow up valuing leadership, independence, and individuality as a result of their parents' willingness to let their kids take risks while simultaneously fostering a sense of security.

Generational Values: New Rules

The oldest Gen Zers are just now, at the time of writing, in their twenties and the youngest haven't left school yet. It's too soon to have a longitudinal perspective on this group, but a cluster of core values stand out: security, security, security. And then pragmatism, stability, achievement, winning, skepticism, individuality, independence, progress, structure, entrepreneurship, privacy, leadership, learning, and creativity. To understand a Gen Zer, follow Greta Thunberg's social media and start watching TikTok videos.

"YOU JUST DON'T UNDERSTAND," SAID BOTH GENERATIONS

If the older generations accuse younger generations of having it too easy and disrespecting the values our elders adhered to, younger generations often blame older generations for creating and bequeathing a less-than-ideal world. Yet, younger generations can overlook how drastically digital media has changed the rules of the game. Before the Internet, it was incredibly difficult to obtain unbiased information (remember encyclopedia sets, anyone?). Today, we can make choices and form opinions and ideas by comparing sources and gathering information instantly. It can be hard to relate to a world where social and political gatekeepers controlled the information everyday folks had access to. And despite Hollywood's incredible efforts to capture the horrors of World War I and World War II (the movie *1917* was bad enough for me), younger generations simply cannot imagine the kind of large-scale, global destruction our older generations experienced. My own grandparents agreed that it was much, much, much worse than what we see on TV. And those acutely and massively challenging situations *do* derail your commitment to your core values faster, stronger, and more easily.

---

54 Howe, Neil. "Meet Mr. and Mrs. Gen X: A New Parent Generation." *The School Superintendents Association (AASA)*, 2010.

HOW CROSS-GEN COMMUNICATION MAKES (Y)OUR WORLD BETTER

If we want to bridge the generational gap, we need to create reasonable pathways for such exchanges to occur. But why bother, you ask? I hear you, apathetic Gen Xers. Because the need for genuine connection holds such an important place in the wellbeing machinery; everyone benefits from the two-way transfer of insight and lessons between our elders and our younger generations. We need each other:

1) To dial down the judgments

We need to know each other so that we can understand or empathize with people outside of our own generation. When we recognize our own generational values and when we understand how other generations acquired theirs, we give ourselves perspective and open ourselves to appreciating people of all ages. We're in this together, seeking genuine fulfillment, and every generation has struggled, survived, and triumphed in their attempts to be fulfilled. When we put ourselves in the shoes of our grandparents, our parents, or our kids, we'll notice that every generation acquired values in response to their particular circumstances. Once we let go of unhelpful stereotypes (too strict, too materialistic, too weak, or too millennial), we'll notice how everyone has always been motivated by what they thought was best for our world. They screwed up, we screwed up, and our kids will likely screw up, but we all share the same ambition: to make the world a safer, healthier, and happier place.

2) To give us a choice

Just as every generation has made choices that have affected the world negatively, every generation has also contributed in ways that have improved society and raised our quality of life. So let's dump the question about which generation is "better" because it does not serve our needs or offer lasting fulfillment. Instead, let's ask, *are my generational values serving me in my life, following my passions and interests, and nurturing my relationships?*

My granddad, part of the civic/silent generation, experienced achievement through the success of his company. My dad, a boomer, talked about achievement as his individual success within his company. I, a millennial, experience achievement through how many people have benefited (become healthier or more motivated) from what I do. And although I am aware that this attitude was—at least in part—shaped by my generation, I choose to continue honoring the value of social service because I get great amount of joy simply from acting on it. In contrast, when I engage with the value of material wealth and the accumulation of status symbols (like a fancy car, a big house with a pool, or a robust investment portfolio), I feel anxious, empty, sluggish, and unmotivated.

3) To become conscious creators of the future

In the past, our collective generational values sprung from necessity, as a *response* to our circumstances. I often catch myself thinking: *What would the world be like if, instead, we could choose our collective values and actively navigate the course of humanity?* In this case, our values wouldn't be acquired, but chosen. And I know—because science has proven this works—the ability to act on or dismiss the values of our own choosing increases our wellbeing.

Thought Experiment: "My Generation"[55]

Here are the questions to help you consider which of your values originate from your generation:

- Go back to the description of your generation and find the generational values that apply to you. Which of them do you feel naturally driven to, and which of them feel like a burden?
- Check out the values of your parents' generation (it might be that you acquired a portion of their values, too) and do the same. Which ones do you enjoy acting on, and which ones feel like obligations (things you *must* or *should* have/be/want)?

---

55 The Who, "My Generation." *My Generation.* Brunswick Records, 1967.

- If a united world government decided which values the world would benefit the most from honoring and passing on to the next generation, what would you add to the list?

Chapter 7

National and Cultural Values

I t had been a long week. When Alicia's parents had flown in from California to spend a week in Spain and meet her new boyfriend, Diego, she'd been positive they'd all have a great time. But everything started to go wrong almost instantly.

On the first night, they met at a fancy restaurant to celebrate Alicia's birthday. Alicia and her parents enjoyed trying the local wine—a lot of it. By the dessert course, Alicia's mom was laughing louder, joking with the staff, and being openly affectionate with Alicia's dad. Alicia was pleased to see her parents relaxing and having a good time. When the time came to pay the bill, Alicia's father offered to split it with Diego. Diego politely refused and paid for everyone.

It wasn't until later in the week when Alicia realized something was off. Diego had opted out of several outings, citing work that Alicia knew he didn't have. He seemed reserved and unwilling to open up around her parents. At home, he was moody and distant, snapping at Alicia over small things. Alicia finally confronted Diego about his behavior. After tears and shouting, Diego admitted that Alicia's parents had made him feel uncomfortable from the start. He objected to Alicia's mother's behavior at the restaurant, saying he was embarrassed by her drinking, loud voice, and laughter in the upscale environment. He pointed out that during the whole week, Alicia's father had only once offered to pick up the check, instead always offering to split it 50/50 with Alicia and Diego. Alicia shrugged, not seeing what the big deal was.

"When your dad asks to split the check with me, I feel insulted and uncomfortable. He is implying that I am too poor to pay for everyone. Plus, as the elder man in the group—if he respects us—*he* should pay more." Alicia stared at Diego, open-mouthed.

"That's definitely *not* what my dad was thinking! He thought he was treating us as equals and being friendly and helpful."

"Well, that's not how it works here!"

Eventually, Diego and Alicia figured out that clashing cultural values were at the bottom of this awkward week. A Spaniard from a well-to-do family, Diego was accustomed to values, such as *tradition, order/structure, formality*, and *respect*. Raised in a society with strict class divisions formalized over centuries, he internalized his culture's more conservative approaches to social interactions and traditions, respecting and honoring unspoken rules about how to treat elders, how to behave as a guest, and what counts as proper public behavior. On the other hand, Alicia and her parents value *equality, openness,* and *informality.* They find value in relaxed approaches to rules and social situations, seeing the rejection of tradition as a way to make people more comfortable.

This makes sense when you consider the differences between American culture and Spanish culture. The USA's understanding of class is based on ideas such as the melting pot and a level playing field, where everyone is (theoretically) given the same chances for success. Hard work— not the class you're born into—determine your social position. In Spain, even to this day, class mobility is difficult, and the legacies of aristocracy still exist in families with noble names and generations of wealth and influence. Furthermore, as a predominantly Catholic country, Spanish culture has long been intertwined with Catholicism's values of *family, rules,* and *tradition.* Meanwhile the radical Protestant roots, which influence American culture, tend to emphasize *individualism* and breaking with traditions and rules perceived as elitist and corrupt. And California has its own unique values, too, being famous for its liberal and laid-back atmosphere.

Once Alicia and Diego figured this out, it was obvious to each of them how the week had been destined for discomfort. The same behavior that Alicia's parents thought was inviting and warm, Diego perceived as insulting and rude.

Although everyone involved had the best intentions, they'd been derailed by different cultural values.

Alicia and Diego's story is a classic example of how important it is for all of us to understand what values we've picked up, consciously or not, from our culture and to ask ourselves if these values are serving us and our wellbeing. If only Alicia and Diego had been taking cultural values coaching.[56]

This is Our Normal

No matter whether they share a border or are separated by oceans, countries across the globe have distinct histories and cultural values, shaped by the unique challenges and advantages each group of people have faced over time. Some countries' histories are intricately tied up in others', while other countries may seem as different as night and day. Wars, migrations, inventions, and climate may all have contributed to prosperity, stagnation, or social regression. As a result, different groups of people have developed varying sets of cultural values, passed down from generation to generation, which form part of our acquired values.

For the purposes of our conversation here, I'll use "culture" and "nation" somewhat interchangeably, with the following caveats: I recognize that one nation can have a variety of different cultures. Similarly, not all cultural groups are sovereign nations, nor are all sovereign groups of people internationally recognized as nations. While borders and cultures *do* change (the history of my own country is a great example of the changing definition of what and who constitutes a "nation"), we can look to a nation's body of literature to identify those values that the citizens have consistently expressed as important. Throughout history, thought leaders have offered observations on their nation's prosperity and stability in the form of legislation, policy papers, works of fiction and poetry, and philosophical treatises. Over time, this body of literature forms the basis for a tribe's beliefs and values.

---

56 Status Update: Eventually, Alicia and Diego *did* do values coaching with me (as their engagement present to each other) and are—through lots of laughs and occasionally some tears—on their way to a better mutual understanding and stronger relationship.

I recently attended a phenomenal talk on diversity given by Dr. Shariff Abdullah, an attorney, author, and advocate for societal transformation. In his talk[57], he gave the best definition of cultural values that I've heard so far:

> *This is a part of our identity we acquired before we acquired the capacity for rational thinking. This is our normal. But we don't even call it normal because it's so normal to us that it's just a background. We refer to it as "reality." And it stays as background until it gets challenged—until you come against a person who has a reality that is different than yours.*

Although we can partially apply this concept to any layer of acquired values, from experience, I can say we're still often more aware of our microenvironmental and generational values simply because we're more exposed to individual differences. For example, we notice differences amongst the families we visit and the advice we're given versus the advice our friends are given, and we definitely notice generational differences. Our national/cultural values, on the other hand, are more stable in our surroundings—especially in our early years—and they set our definition of "normal."

Because we lack *true* awareness of our national and cultural values (let alone others'), we almost never consider what would happen if we rejected or embraced different national/cultural values when moving around the globe in our quest for fulfillment, experience, success, or better lives in general. We often fail to plan for scenarios in which our personal values don't match the environment we're in. But because I've been there done that, I can tell you that understanding your cultural/national values is as important as renewing your passport. I, however, had to learn the hard way . . .

My Normal

I learned the most about the process of reprograming our value system and priorities from my own experience with nationally- and culturally-acquired

---

57 Abdullah, Dr. Shariff. "'Solutions Beyond Diversity': Understanding Invisible, Implicit and Assumed Cultures." WBECS, 2019. Full Summit, included with permission from the author.

values. There were some national values so deeply coded in my value system that I thought they *must* be absolute truths. Learning that they were "only" my acquired values was a life-changing experience for me.

Let me tell you more about this. As you already know by now, I was born in Yugoslavia in the early eighties. What I have always loved the most about my country of origin are the people—always open, always generous, and always friendly. But when I talk about my tribe, I'm biased. So, I'm going to share a part of an article about Serbia from one of my favorite websites, *Culture Trip*, which deals with different cultures, diversity, and helping world travelers better understand the places they intend to visit:

> Serbia is a nation of incredible nature, passionate nightlife and monumental history, but most visitors come away from the country with one very important aspect at the top of their 'Reasons I Love Serbia' list. That would be the Serbs themselves, of course. The people make the country, and that is particularly true in a state that has spent most of the last two decades being frequently demonized. Serbs are a rare breed, unique in some incredible ways, and boy do we love them.
>
> Here is why.
>
> The entire Balkan region is renowned for its hospitality, and the Serbs are well and truly a part of this. If you find yourself lucky enough to be invited into the home of a local person, our advice is to prepare properly by not eating for a day and not planning anything for the day after. You will likely be plied with food and drink until there is nothing left, regardless of the financial position of your host. The Serbs will go out of their way to make sure a good time is had by all, and nothing is going to get in the way of that. There is such a thing as too much hospitality, but don't tell the Serbs that.[58]

Need Help? Stay for Dinner

I could fill a book with my own examples supporting *Culture Trip's* commentary. Here's just one: Once, I was spending my summer vacation on a mountain in central Serbia, Kopaonik. My friend and I went hiking, and we lost

58   Bills, John William. "11 Reasons Why We Love Serbia's People." *Culture Trip*, 2017.

track of time, totally absorbed by the natural beauty and stunning views. When it began to get dark, we figured we were at least a three-hour walk away from our hotel. But we didn't panic; we knew all we had to do was ask for help. We walked half a mile to the first village. We leaned over the fence of the first house we saw and asked an older man, who was working in his garden, where we could find a local bus to reach our hotel.

"Just come in for a coffee, and I will give you a map and detailed directions," he said and continued to his wife, "Milanka, please put some coffee on the stove; we have guests."

The older lady was thrilled to have us, and we had a very friendly conversation over a cup of a delicious home-brewed coffee. We learned they had a son about our age, that he's studying in Belgrade and that they loved our hometown of Novi Sad but haven't visited it in a while. And that they will definitely have to do it soon because their favorite singer was having a concert there next year. When we wanted to leave and catch the bus, the old man said, "Absolutely no way." He pointed toward the oven from where smells of the traditional Serbian dinner—*burek*—wafted tantalizingly toward us. So we stayed for the dinner and chatted for another two hours until Milanka said, "Petre, we will bring them to their hotel, right? It's just too dark now, and I will enjoy a short ride to the city." When the time to split ways came, *they* thanked *us* for the great evening and wished us all the best for the future. Where I grew up, situations like this one were *normal*.

Dear Senka, This is Not Normal. Love, Austria

Then, in my mid-twenties, I moved to Graz, Austria, to pursue a PhD in molecular medicine. Although I was only 350 miles away from home, the cultural differences stunned me. Imagine a twenty-five-year old me, used to "too much hospitality," moving to a country whose immigrants often describe it as "one of the least approachable nationalities" they've encountered so far.

One of the first things foreigners in Austria notice is how hesitant locals are in getting to know people. In her quest to prepare me for what was coming, my colleague from the PhD program, who had relocated to Austria a year ahead of me, described it as feeling invisible all of the time:

It's difficult to pick up conversations. When they get in an elevator, a bus, tram, or train, they avoid eye contact, clutch their phone, and pretend they're not surrounded by twenty other people in an enclosed space. It's impossible to say they are a mean and cold-hearted nation, but as compared to dozens of other nationalities, they very rarely go the extra mile to help out a stranger (and among us, they have, by far, the worst customer service—very rude and downright mean sometimes).

I hate to say this, but this is how I felt for most of my first five years in Austria, with a disclaimer that this holds true mainly for the cities—there is a huge and well-documented socio-cultural city/country divide. I found it very difficult to make meaningful connections with locals, and even when I had, over time, forged friendships (as opposed to *colleague* or *acquaintance*), I missed the spontaneity, openness, and casualness of Serbs. Everything felt too formal. I would attend a dinner at friend's place and, as we departed, they would take out their little calendar notebook and ask me which date would be appropriate to see each other again (in about four to six weeks, ideally), which made me feel as if any interaction before that specified date would be unwelcome.

Grand Theft Auto, Serbian Edition

I have also witnessed the reverse of this particular culture clash when traveling in Serbia with Austrians. Once, while visiting my hometown of Novi Sad, I watched my Austrian brother-in-law struggle with "too much hospitality" in combination with the popular stereotype that Serbia—really all of Eastern Europe—is dangerous and lawless, prime spots for auto theft. Indeed, when he announced to his colleagues that he's planning to visit Serbia, their first reaction was, "Hopefully not with *your* car!"

I wanted to make this vacation great, and I wanted him not to worry, so I asked a friend of mine with a secured, locked, and surveyed parking garage if my brother-in-law could leave his car there. When we reached Novi Sad, we immediately drove there to leave his car. My friend's mom was waiting for us, happy that they could help us. In a totally open, Serbian manner, she said, "I apologize. My husband was in an extreme rush this morning and parked his car in a way that doesn't leave much room for you. But don't bother, just leave me your car keys, and when my husband is back, he will move his car and park yours, and you can collect the keys anytime tomorrow."

I happily replied "Sure." For me, it was the most logical thing to do in this situation. But then I saw my brother-in-law's thunderstruck face. He was in a total panic. And I knew he was thinking, "Oh my gosh, it's happening. I've been here for half an hour, and they want my car keys—surely this is one of their tricks, and I'll never see my car again."

Visibly uncomfortable, he stuttered awkwardly, "Let's go and check the lot; maybe I can park . . ." And you know what? The three Austrian fellows got the car into the tight spot. It only took them sixty-seven back and forths, but the car was in. And, most importantly, the key was in my brother-in-law's pocket.

But the story doesn't stop there. As he left his car "secured," we urgently needed to get a taxi because we were late for dinner. During the ride, the driver and I started an informal conversation about where we were from, what we are doing in Novi Sad, how long we are going to stay, ending with his personal tips on what not to miss while in town. When we left his vehicle, my sister-in-law said, "So nice that you met with an old friend of yours."

First, I was confused, but then I got it. From our tone of voice, body language, and his interest in helping us, she was sure I knew the driver and that he was a good friend of mine. I giggled, "I don't know that guy. Just saw him for the first time in my life." She was utterly surprised.

"Seriously? And you talk just like that about your personal stuff with a complete stranger?"

Culture Clashes with Wellbeing

Swapping stories about culture clash can be fun at parties and is a particular kind of bonding between different outsiders who have found themselves in the same unfamiliar place. But there's more to these stories than your classic fish-out-of-water comedy.

Although you may laugh, such situations can be very frustrating if you are alone and unfamiliar with your new cultural environment. I was always used to starting a conversation when I sit next to someone on public transportation, on a plane, or in taxis. When I moved to Graz, I, of course, acted in my usual, open way. And I felt rejected all the time.

When I was developing the concept of different layers of acquired values, I asked myself what values might contribute to Serbian/Yugoslavian identity and culture. To discover these values, I had to go back and look at the time when the country was thriving the most, and what important lessons persist as legacies from those times. I reviewed what I learned in my history classes and what situations were labeled as key moments for Serbian history. One of them is definitely the break of the Syrmian Front, an Axis line of defense during World War II. When I finally looked at my values, behaviors and struggles through the lens of these stories, I experienced one of my greatest "aha" moments of all time.

Brotherhood and Unity

On April 6, 1941, the Axis powers attacked the Kingdom of Yugoslavia from all directions. As they comprised of forces from almost every neighboring country (Italy, Hungary, and Bulgaria, altogether lead by Germany), the inevitable unconditional surrender of the Yugoslav Army followed in only ten days. The terms of the defeat were brutal: Axis members dismembered Yugoslavia and divided its territory. And not only in a geographical sense—they also heated the tensions among ex-compatriots by creating divisive "us" versus "them" ideologies among the many national, ethnic, and religious groups of Yugoslavia.

The early resistance, the army of the Communist Party known as the Partisans, was inspired by the idea of fighting the occupying forces and creating a multi-cultural state of Yugoslavia. Fairly small and poorly armed formation underwent nationwide uprising because its sympathizers gathered around common ideology and not ethnic interests, thereby acquiring support from all parts of the country. Their leader, Josip Broz Tito, used an empowering slogan, "Brotherhood and Unity," to promote the power of united Yugoslavia in its fight against the fascist enemy. Tito's message was so clear that it wiped away any trace of provincialism: Serbs and Croats and Slovenes, Macedonians, Bosnians, Christian, Muslim, Orthodox, and Catholic must shelf their differences, if they are to sustain any chance of winning the war.[59]

---

59 Davidson, Basil. *Partisan Picture*. New York City: Bedford Books, 1946.

To safely evacuate the German army from the Balkans, the Axis powers established the Syrmian Front in October 1944. Supported by their Soviet allies, the Partisans endured fierce winter battles to finally break the Syrmian Front exactly four years after they were defeated by the invasion of the Axis powers. The Yugoslav Army then freed the entire territory of occupied Yugoslavia in under a month.

"Yugoslav nations jointly led a national liberation war. If they were not united, they wouldn't have won. Brotherhood and unity are the biggest strengths and the highest values of the Yugoslav Army," Tito said after the victory. His celebrated slogan "Brotherhood and Unity" evolved into a guiding principle of post-war Yugoslavia.

One of the hallmarks of Yugoslavia's post-war advancement, rooted in the principle of brotherhood and unity, are "youth labor actions"—voluntary labor by young people organized to build public infrastructure, such as roads, railways, and public buildings, as well as industrial infrastructure. The country's largest highway connecting four constituent republics of former Yugoslavia was one of their best-known projects.

A Youth Labor Brigade[60]

---

60 This Slovene work is in the public domain in its source country and the United
    States because its copyright expired pursuant to the Yugoslav Copyright Act of 1978, which
    provided for copyright term of the life of the author plus fifty years, respectively twenty-five
    years since the publication for photographs and works of applied art.

I still remember my history class glorifying the power of the united labor of volunteers: "A first section between Zagreb and Belgrade, built with the effort of volunteer Youth Labor Brigades, opened in 1950. The section between Ljubljana and Zagreb was built by the joint effort of 54,000 volunteers in less than eight months in 1958."[61] And can you guess the name of this highway? Of course, "The Brotherhood and Unity Highway" (not a joke).

I also clearly remember (although, it was more than twenty-five years ago) one episode of the most influential children's educational TV shows, "Cube, Cube, Cubelet," which aired for several decades in Yugoslavia. The main character of the show was Branko Kockica (Branko the Cubelet), who, with a group of preschoolers, explored the human environment and everyday life. The show also offered lessons on how to behave and be a good friend. In one episode[62], Branko Kockica faced the question, "What is Yugoslavia?"

"We are small but united country," he said. "We have to stick together because some strong, economically powerful country can easily break us." At this point, he looked around and saw the confused faces of the children. "I see you all stare at me; you don't really get what I'm talking about, right? Let me try this way—how many states has our country?"

"Our country has six states," said one little boy.

Branko found seven branches and gave one to the boy. "Imagine you are one powerful, strong country, and you want to break this lonely Serb. Or a lonely Croat. Try it."

The boy broke the branch with little effort. Then, Branko bound six branches together and said to the boy, "Imagine you are the world's most powerful country. Try now. Try really hard. Imagine you are the most powerful space force from Venus. Try really, really hard. Or imagine you are the strongest Martian. It's not working, ha?"

The boy gave up and looked at his lightly scratched palms.

"If all of us from all six states stick together . . . if we help each other, then we are strong, then we are unbreakable. Nobody can break united brothers. That is Yugoslavia."

61 Ljiljana, Kovačević. *Jugoslavija 1941–1981*. Beograd: Eksport Press, 1981.
62 "Branko Kockica Jugoslavija." June 3, 2013. Video, 3:52. https://www.youtube.com/watch?v=9ahtP2QAvlA.

Other kids tried to break the bunch of brunches, but no one managed.

"So what did we learn today?" asked Branko.

"Together we are stronger! Unity saves us," replied the children.

When I consider these examples, it comes as no surprise that people in Serbia and the Balkan region tend to stick together and help others without hesitation. If I look back, our national anthem, our emblem (it is alleged the fire steels in the national emblem are acronyms for "only unity saves the Serbs"), and everything we ever learned about our past, they all glorify the principle of brotherhood and unity.

Frau Doktor Holzer?

When I applied for—and received—permanent residence in Austria after it became obvious my Austrian husband and I would raise our family here, I also caught a glimpse at Austrian history and national heritage. It was time for me to finally and wholeheartedly embrace the mentality of my new homeland.

Before I studied for the official exam in Austrian history organized by the immigration office, many things in this country felt strange to me. Apart from feeling rejected all of the time, due to Austrians' frigid approach to personal interactions and their "protocol" for respectfully getting to know each other by keeping a distance, there were two other things that repeatedly bothered me. First, their obsession with titles. For example, your doctoral degree is documented everywhere: in your passport, on your credit card, on your doorbell, and, as the ultimate culmination, on your tombstone. If they call your turn, for example, at the doctor's office or in the bank, they will always address you with *Frau (or Herr) Doktor*. In Serbia on the other hand, I don't think it is even legal to write your title on official documents as the part of your name, and it is certainly seen as bragging if you stress your title in your everyday life. Another foreign friend of my doing a post-doc in Graz agreed with me. She told me that her Austrian mentor even advised her to always use her *Frau Doktor* title if she wanted to be respected and receive efficient service. A laidback native Californian used to informality, she found the protocol uncomfortable—even a bit arrogant.

Where are You From?

How much I hated this question in my early years in Austria. It always reminded me that I don't (already) belong here. After some time, I realized it has something to do with the second thing that bothered me: I had a feeling that Austrians only like Austrians. They take pride in stressing their Austrian origin and are especially proud of their history (Holy Habsburg Empire, Batman!), their geniuses (composers like Mozart, Strauss, and Haydn; or scientists like Sigmund Freud and Gregor Mendel, to name a few), and their beautiful landscape and clean cities. To non-Austrians, Austrians can appear to act self-sufficient, superior, and as if they look down at other nations.

So those were some impressions about Austrians and Austrian culture I had as I began to study for my residency exam. The first thing I noticed about my exam preparation guide was that out of thirty-something pages about Austrian history, a large portion was dedicated to the Habsburg Empire, especially the important role of Maria Theresia, the only female ruler of the Habsburg territories and the last of the House of Habsburg. The government team that wrote the "integration manual" made sure potential residents would remember that Austria was the most powerful empire in Europe in the eighteenth century. During the reign of Maria Theresia, significant reforms, which had lasting effects, were implemented. Austria's military and bureaucratic reforms strengthened their efficiency, while financial reforms greatly improved the economy by doubling the state revenue in only ten years. Under Maria Theresia, compulsory education was introduced for the first time, textbooks were standardized, and control of all schools in the country was introduced. Her dedication to order, application of rules, education, and culture have become synonymous for national success and have been distilled into Austrian society's most important national values. It is, therefore, not at all surprising that Austrians worship their academic titles and that—due to their countless innovations and contributions to culture and scientific discoveries— they take pride in their ancestors' superior contribution to society's progress.

No Mother, No Cry

But Austria's more recent history is also imprinted in their national and cultural values. You remember the parenting manual *The German Mother and*

Her First Child from the previous chapter? [Note: Austria and Germany united during this period, so "German mother" also applied to "Austrian mother."] When women's husbands were fighting in the field far away from home and families, the toughness propagated by Haarer could have acutely helped coping with the horrors of the war and loses and could actually have been comforting in some ways. But in the long run, this approach caused many emotional troubles—and it still does—according to research greatly analyzed by German psychologist Anne Kratzer.

One aspect of Haarer's ideas is particularly imprinted in German values today: Haarer pushed mothers to let their babies "manage" their emotional needs on their own to promote *strength* and *self-reliance*. Deeply believing that those values are ultimate assets, many German parents (in contrast to other Western countries) still think it's a positive sign if your baby or toddler doesn't cry when the mother leaves the room.[63]

When Anne interviewed Klaus Grossmann, an authority in the field of mother-child attachment, he shared that he repeatedly observed scenes like this, both in his experimental settings and in real life: A baby or a toddler gets upset and starts crying. The mother instinctively runs toward her to make sure she's not physically hurt but suddenly stops moving just in front of her child. She then neither picks the baby up, nor soothes her.

When the researchers from Grossmann's team asked the mothers why they didn't pick up their babies and comfort them, they overwhelmingly agreed they didn't want to spoil them. But it's not all about the mothers. "An Indian feels no pain"—an idiom essentially meaning, "Be as stoic as a Native American"—is often heard in Austria and Germany today,[64] especially by fathers and grandfathers who equally glorify strength and toughness and who try to infuse it into their offspring's value system, both when they're deadly serious or when they're (seemingly) joking.

For a long time, I couldn't understand what makes Austrians (or Germans) so different. How is it possible that they see allowing others to get close to them

---

63   Anne Kratzer, Erziehung für den Führer; Gehirn&Geist 5/2018, Approved for citation purposes by *Spektrum der Wissenschaft Verlags GmbH 2021*

64   Anne Kratzer, Erziehung für den Führer; Gehirn&Geist 5/2018, Approved for citation purposes by *Spektrum der Wissenschaft Verlags GmbH 2021*

as a sign of weakness, while people from the Balkans see it as the only way to thrive (and survive)? Now, with all pieces of puzzle I have collected over the years, including all the family stories I've heard, my inner response is . . . *It couldn't be any other way.*

THE DOUBLE-EDGED SWORD

Getting to know another culture, accept it, and finally embrace it is only half of the story. My biggest takeaway from my attempts to understand and integrate into Austrian culture was, for the first time in my life, the opportunity to consider the negative side of some of my own national values. Once I was paying attention, I noticed how some of my national values actually clashed with some of my core values, without me even noticing.

"Brotherhood and unity" are great values to rely on when you ask a friend whether or not you can stay in her city apartment during spring break. Or if you need an hour's ride to the airport at 4:00 a.m. on Sunday morning. But a reliance on informal hospitality and generosity also means it's okay to ask your cardiologist friend if your grandmother can come for a checkup without an appointment . . . or your judge friend if she can speed up probate proceedings . . . or your friend, the dean of the university, if your son can get a research assistant position without an official application process.

During my last vacation in Novi Sad (after ten years of living abroad), I was mildly disturbed by the stories of my friends, who almost proudly reported how excited they were to have found a connection to smooth the enrollment of their child into kindergarten or the music or elementary school of their choice. In a country like Austria, where people value order and the application of rules, things don't normally work this way. I would feel embarrassed to call someone and ask for privileged treatment, even though I have been working in the State Hospital for the last thirteen years. When my husband and I applied for the public daycare services for our boy, we didn't worry if he'd "get in" or not because the criteria are clear, public, and you can follow the selection procedure. Also, due to the high value placed on order and culture, the entire country fulfills an OCD's standards of cleanliness. I travel a lot for work and family visits, and as soon as I cross the border into Austria, I have a feeling that everything becomes more organized—the fields, the streets, the tunnels, and the parking lots. I like Austrian order. I like how they *willingly* follow the rules because they collectively value order. It's easier to trust their system, and I feel safer here. And, I hate to admit this: the last two things I couldn't really say for the country I come from.

What I learned on my journey is that there is always a tradeoff. For our Serbian openness, we have more general trust in people; we are more closely connected to each other. A friend of a friend is automatically your friend, as well. You can count on others to help you in the middle of the night even when it's inconvenient. Your need for relatedness is more genuinely and more easily satisfied in the surrounding like this. But your need for autonomy or competence can easily suffer in a "friendship economy." You may be the best and most qualified candidate for your dream job, but you may never get it because a friend of a friend is in line before you.

A WORD OR TWO ON AMERICAN VALUES

During my postdoctoral years, I lived for two years in California. Want to know my take on American values?

When I got a postdoc position at University of California, Davis, my first step was to obtain a work visa. Along with all the paperwork and forms to fill out, I also got a sheet from the Integration Office, offering the list of national values summarized by Marian Beane, the former Director of the International Student/Scholar Office on the campus of the University of North Carolina in Charlotte.[65] This is the (shortened) list:

Individuality: US Americans are encouraged at an early age to be independent and develop their own goals in life. They are encouraged to not depend (too much) on others, including their friends, teachers, and parents.

Equality: US Americans uphold the ideal that everyone "is created equal" and has the same rights. This includes women as well as men of all ethnic and cultural groups living in the US.

---

65   "An Adventure in American Culture and Values." UNC-Charlotte, accessed 10 Feb 2021, https://www.internationalstudentguidetotheusa.com/articles/culture.php, included with permission from the author.

Efficiency: US Americans take pride in making the best use of their time. In the business world, "time is money." Being "on time" for class, an appointment, or for dinner with your host family is important.

Informality: The US American lifestyle is generally casual. You will see students going to class in shorts and t-shirts. Male instructors seldom wear a tie, and female instructors often wear comfortable walking shoes.

Achievement & Hard Work/Play: The foreign visitor is often impressed at how achievement-oriented Americans are and how hard they both work and play. A competitive spirit is often the motivating factor to work harder.

It's easy to align this list of national values with American history and the country's foundational texts, such as the *Declaration of Independence* and the *Bill of Rights.* From the beginning, Americans focused on the (hard-working, property-owning) individual, as opposed to society at large. The opening sentence of the Declaration of Independence sums up the story America likes to tell about itself: "We hold these truths to be self-evident, that all men are created equal, that they are endowed by their Creator with certain unalienable rights that among these are Life, Liberty and the Pursuit of Happiness." As a result, American culture rewards *individualism.* In its founding rhetoric, it admires people who are different, *hardworking achievers* who have the *courage* to create their own destiny, who forge their own paths.

My own experience mostly confirmed what the US government told me to expect. I found no problems with a "friendship economy," one of the biggest need-thwarting issues in Serbia, nor did I encounter reserved and distant people, one of the biggest need-thwarting issues in Austria. But before you conclude American national values are perfect, let me add an observation.

Due to the high value Americans place on *individuality, efficiency,* and *achievement*, people can be *too* work-oriented, even in the situations that require slowing down. For example, something that was very relevant to me—and few of my close American friends—at the time of my stay in California was maternity leave. The American process of maternity leave and return to work was deeply unsettling. I wondered how it felt to be an American working mom, especially a first-time mom. You are expected to bounce back as if nothing really happened and re-enter the workforce only weeks after you gave birth. You might even be among the 25 percent of American mothers who return to work two weeks postpartum, even before your baby can support her head on her own. You are expected to have all the issues, such as your body, your childcare, your emotions (including baby blues or postnatal depression), and, most of all, your mind under control. That is crazy. And it is very detrimental for your need for relatedness—paradoxically—with your own newborn baby who is also naturally hardwired to build the strongest attachment to you.

My recent maternity leave experience as a working mom in Austria couldn't be more different. (Disclaimer: I am not trying to turn anyone green with envy.) First, let's talk about *Mutterschutz*, which literally means, "mother protection." This names the period of eight weeks before and eight to twelve weeks after your due date when you are legally not allowed to work—even if you want to. And the state will pay every single woman with Austrian residence—no matter her citizenship, religion, or employment status—either 100 percent of her salary or the minimum wage if she's unemployed. After this period, she will get one year of regular maternity leave, with 80 percent of her salary. If you are unemployed, the state will also cover your stay in the hospital and, if needed, you will be provided with an obstetrician, a breastfeeding specialist, a psychologist, and a physiotherapist.

If you are a working mom in Serbia, whose economy is in much worse of a state than either the US or Austria, you will get fifty-two weeks of 100 percent of your salary (unless working in the Private Sector, but that's a whole other story) to take care of your baby. And you will get support from your family and friends like almost nowhere else in the world.

It is clear that the Austrian, and especially the Serbian economy, would be better off if they didn't provide such benefits to working moms (ah well, at least in the short run). But it is the *choice* of the people. They elect, over and over, a government that chooses to value family over the speediest economic growth. People are aware they will raise their family in the 650-square-foot apartment with one bathroom, they will drive one—probably used—family car, and they may not have enough money to afford a dog or exotic destinations in summer. I believe people in Europe vote for different policies than Americans because they don't value *individuality, efficiency,* and *achievement* (as they are defined in my brochure) as much as Americans.

A Word or Two On Chinese Values

Like every decent Ping-Pong player, I was obsessed with China in my childhood years. It was a dream come true for me when I could spend a summer hitting the ball in different parts of China—in Beijing, Shanghai, and the coastal region of south China. I was seventeen, and I noticed more differences than similarities in the new culture I was immersed in. It felt like another planet.

Now, as an adult (and values enthusiast), I understand that Chinese culture is different from mine because it has been shaped by different histories and influenced by different foundational writings. If you were born and raised in Mainland China, your value system would be under the strong influence of the writings of Confucius, Buddha, and Mao Tse-Tung.[66] For centuries, Chinese people celebrated and promoted *conformity*. They have a saying that captures this value: "If the nail stands out, pound it down." Why does Chinese culture value conformity so much more than, let's say, American culture? Because twenty-five centuries ago, Confucius, one of the most influential philosophers in entire Chinese history, contributed to the country's prosperity and peace preservation by urging people to obey the interests of the nation rather than focusing on one's own individuality. Confucius's writings help explain why the Chinese admire *conformity, humility, modesty, patience,* and *tradition,* and astonishingly, they do so even 2,500 years after Confucius's death.

A more recent phase in Chinese history was a form of communism, supported and promoted by Mao Tse-Tung. Although Communism brought some questionable stuff, it had one thing in common with the teachings of Confucius: The wellbeing of the group—society—is more important than the individual. Communism spread like a plague in China, further cementing cultural and societal values of the most populous country in the world.

Today, you can see the powerful combination of Confucius's and Communism's influence on Chinese culture in a variety of ways. For example, I noticed the extreme modesty of Chinese people. My Chinese host family and

---

66 Hedges, Burke. "Read and Grow Rich." *I N T I Pub & Resource Books Inc.,* 1999.

friends were uncomfortable putting themselves forward, receiving individual compliments or accolades, or appearing to seek too much individual attention.

TRAVEL FAR, MEET YOURSELF

The British novelist David Mitchell wrote in his best-selling novel, *Cloud Atlas,* that if you travel far enough, you'll meet yourself.[67] Did Mitchell reach into my soul to come up with these words? Or maybe he also read the brilliant study from Rice University, in conjunction with Columbia University and the University of North Carolina (UNC), which found that people who relocate to a new country tend to have a better sense of self than those who don't.[68] Or maybe, just maybe, I'm not the only one profoundly changed by my cross-cultural experiences?

The researchers from Rice, Columbia, and UNC conducted six studies involving 1,874 participants enrolled into MBA programs in the US, and they compared those who lived abroad versus those who did not. The team found that when people could reflect about themselves in the context of new and different cultures, they were much better in discovering which values and norms truly define who they are and which merely reflect their cultural upbringing.

The team even noted that relocating to the new country is associated with greater life satisfaction, decreased stress, and improved job performance—all because living abroad influences one's self-concept, including individual's strengths and values, by enhancing its clarity.[69] The authors conclude and I fully concur—the shortest path to know *your* values and make right choices for *yourself* leads around the world!

BE A FORCE FOR GOOD

In each and every part of this book, I'm not advocating for you to drop your acquired cultural values. Just imagine for a moment a world in which we didn't have cultural and national values that we shared with others. We would go

67   Mitchell, David. "Cloud Atlas." *Sceptre,* 2014.
68   Adam, Hajo, Obodaru, Otilia, et. al. "The Shortest Path to Oneself Leads Around the World: Living Abroad Increases Self-Concept Clarity." *Organizational Behavior and Human Decision Processes,* 2018.
69   Adam, Hajo, Obodaru, Otilia, et. al. "The Shortest Path to Oneself Leads Around the World: Living Abroad Increases Self-Concept Clarity."

around acting *solely* in unique, individual, and idiosyncratic ways. It would be difficult to recognize other members of "our tribe," bond with, and understand each other. And we wouldn't feel safe in situations where we don't know what to expect or how to predict how others might react.

But, at the same time, we are much more likely than our ancestors to interact with people who don't share our national or cultural values. Globalization has created opportunities to work, live, study, and pursue relationships in other countries, while war, instability, terror, suffering economies, and hunger pull people away from their homes.

That's why I'm inviting you to imagine what humanity could accomplish on a grand scale if we could collectively raise our awareness around our national and cultural values and practice cultural humility while simultaneously deeply respecting our heritage. Beyond increasing our personal satisfaction (as I was lucky enough to experience), we might have a chance at reducing conflict and working consciously for the wellbeing of all.

> *How are we supposed to treat others?*
> "There are no others."
> —Ramana Maharshi

Thought Experiment: Where Do You Come From?

- **To understand the power of the written word, take a moment to reflect on the culture in which you were raised.** Was it part of a larger, national culture, or was the culture you were raised in different from the national culture surrounding you? Write down whatever you know about your culture's/nation's history, especially when the country was prospering. Think about the prominent manuscripts that likely influenced generations. Feel free to do some research if your history classes were a long time ago. Images from times of prosperity are particularly powerful. **What cultural values do you and your "tribe" hold?**

- **Think of your personal experiences with different cultures.** Have you traveled extensively or lived abroad? Where? Are you or someone close to you in a multicultural marriage or relationship? Have you worked or studied closely with someone from another culture? What cultural differences are you aware of? What political, geographic, or religious factors might have influenced people's values?

Chapter 8
Expectation-Reality Gap

W hen external sources "teach" us what to value, they—without exception—promise an attractive reward if we follow their advice. Most commonly, we learn that we'll achieve a "good" and "happy" life if we do certain things and avoid doing other things. We work hard at meeting values-driven goals and expect happiness as promised. But, as we all know, meeting goals does not always produce the sustained intense happiness we expect.

This doesn't mean that everyone and everything in the world is out to get us, feeding us false information to set us up for disappointment. Our parents, guardians, and teachers have only the best intentions when they transfer their values to us. But due to our unique "psychological DNA," the promised results often fail to become realized. We find ourselves missing that rich feeling of inner self-worth. I call this effect **the "Expectation-Reality Gap."**

My research shows that we are more likely to experience an Expectation-Reality Gap if our acquired values, rather than our core values, drive the goals we've set. Even those acquired values that we absorb from our loving parents may or may not be serving us. As you've (hopefully!) seen by now, our individual core values may differ significantly from our parents' or social trends in certain key areas. That's why we may spend years or even decades "climbing the ladder only to find out it's leaning against the wrong wall."[70]

---

70   This quote is commonly attributed to Thomas Merton and Stephen R. Covey.

BUILDING A SNOWBALL (EFFECT)

In scientific language, we say that there is a strong correlation between happiness and achieving a goal based on a core value. That means there is very little gap between expectation and reality (*see the graph on the left*). Goals based on acquired values have a strong correlation with happiness at first but then quickly drops, creating an increasingly larger Expectation-Reality Gap (*see the graph on the right*).

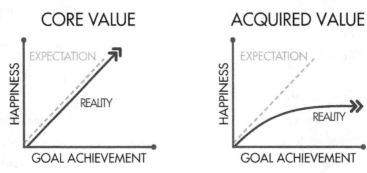

If we're chasing external values that are not aligned with our core values, even when we reach a goal—the university degree, the job, the award, or the new house—the payoff is brief and less than we expected. Although the instant spikes of satisfaction may be very intense, they quickly fade, making a life based on acquired values a life full of peaks and valleys. On the other hand, our core values can unlock our most powerful resource—our intrinsic motivation—and make us feel satisfied on the deepest level. Core values build on each other for a lasting effect of happiness. You get more and more and more fulfilled.

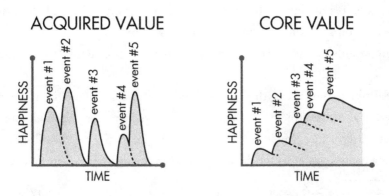

My own life offers ample proof that the fulfillment from pursuing my core values builds and builds over time. Although being successful in an academic career certainly gives me a feeling of competence on many occasions, it drastically differs from the feeling I get when I work on my core value of *motivation*. Academic success gives me intensive, but short-living spikes of happiness that fade away with the next challenge. Today, when I think of an academic award that I received some years ago, it has only little, if any, meaning for me. In contrast, the competence I feel from motivating others provides me with lasting satisfaction; it gives me energy and a sense of purpose in life, even years after the "motivation-moment" took place.

"STRANGERS IN THE NIGHT"[71]

The day after I had my second baby, I was exhausted. Those who have #twoundertwo at home know what level of exhaustion I'm talking about. My baby finally fell asleep, and I was about to do the same when I heard quiet sobbing from my roommate's bed. For a short second, I wanted to close my eyes and pretend that I didn't hear her. I was desperate for a few hours of sleep. But I just couldn't let her cry alone in a strange hospital room.

"It's OK to be scared . . ." I whispered.

A first-time mom, my roommate had prematurely given birth to her little daughter, and she was full of fear and despair. I could only imagine what she was going through. So, we talked and talked, cried and laughed, and I let her vent and share all of her concerns. We brainstormed the name for her little warrior baby girl. It was 5:00 a.m. when we decided to get some sleep. My baby was awake at 5:30 a.m., but my heart was so full of the positive change I witnessed in those few hours, I didn't feel tired—not the tiniest bit. And the joy of being there for my roommate didn't wear off many years after (you should see me smiling while writing this).

Satisfying our needs through acting on our core values is much more powerful and effective than pursuing goals based on our acquired values. It carries a deeper meaning for us. Like a great engine in the middle of our chests, our core values power us for the long haul. On the flip side, when we chase our

---

71   Frank Sinatra. "Strangers in the Night." *Strangers in the Night.* Studio album, 1966.

acquired values, we may disengage that strong engine and find ourselves losing power and momentum over time—until we simply run out of gas.

What about you? Can you remember helping someone or someone helping you some years ago? How did it feel then? How does it feel now? (I know you're smiling.)

FIND YOUR SET POINT: MO' MONEY, MO' PROBLEMS

Some acquired values serve us well, even though they are acquired. Also, some values can have both core and acquired traits. For example, we can truly value an attribute, behavior, or condition but may feel so pressured by our environment to incessantly strive for more of it that the value no longer feels natural. In both cases, the problem is not the value itself but the pressure we feel to constantly exhibit it—and to exhibit a lot of it. In such situations, I suggest you spend some time assessing what scientists call the value's *set point*—the point after which the achieved amount of the goals only marginally affects your happiness.

ACQUIRED VALUE

One of the most famous "set point" examples is money—the level of income after which more money no longer brings proportional boosts of happiness. In the beginning, our happiness grows as our bank account grows. So, it makes sense that we may pursue materialistic goals at the beginning of our careers. It also explains why people who have less find genuine satisfaction in earning more. But then the curve flattens, and we need large sums of money to induce only small increases in our genuine satisfaction.

Being able to accurately assess the "sweet spot" where our efforts optimally meet our fulfillment is one of the most valuable tools in your My Best Life toolbox. After the set point, the Expectation-Reality Gap only gets bigger and bigger, and it may bring frustration (sometimes seen as a slight drop in happiness) with it. Everything we do to achieve goals beyond the "set point" quickly drains our energy in two ways. First, achieving these goals requires effort, and second, we can end up blaming ourselves for neglecting what matters most when our desire to exhibit an acquired value goes unchecked. As the gap grows, the ache inside us grows, as well. And we feel the need to respond.

MIND THE GAP

We typically respond to Expectation-Reality Gaps in two ways: we try even harder or we reject the value.

Scenario 1: Going Above and Beyond

Because a short boost of joy after achieving a goal based on our acquired value can be quite intense, our instincts tell us that for greater satisfaction and longer effect, we need to work harder to gain more of the same thing. Thus, we initially respond by going above and beyond. We try harder, investing more time and resources. As we invest more time and energy pursuing a single value, we pay a high cost—not enough emotional bandwidth to support other values in our system. If prolonged, this scenario may result in extreme behaviors that can cause us to either burn out or neglect others.

Rebel With A(n) (Acquired) Cause

When he was fourteen years old, Michi's (hubs again) teacher had a meeting with his parents and told them, "He'll never graduate from school" and "It would be better if he just goes back to the farm and helps out." For the record, he was a terrible student at the time (his words). He clogged the sink and let the water overflow during physics, he played cards during German lessons, and during religion class, he was nowhere to be seen, usually drinking beer with the other two rebels.

His mom agreed with Michi's teacher, but Michi's dad insisted that he stay. He told his son that he'd never go anywhere in life without a high school diploma. So Michi not only finished high school, he graduated from college with a degree in chemistry, earned a Master's in Biochemistry at ETH Zürich (yes, that ETH), and he earned his PhD from the Medical University of Graz (you got that right . . . we met at the job interview). But these days, Michi has a different perspective on his unexpected academic success: "Short-term, I enjoyed how I grew in the eyes of the society after every title I earned, only to figure out that in the long-term, the only thing that really grew was the dissatisfaction inside me."

Scenario 2: Reject the Value

When an Expectation-Reality Gap gets too wide, and we conclude that a specific value will bring us only worry and frustration, we might eventually reject the value completely. Outright rejection can be the "gateway drug" for a whole host of negative feelings—anger, resentment, blaming, avoidance, and despair. We might reject not only the value itself but also anyone and anything associated with it. In the most extreme case, we might take on behaviors that directly oppose the value.

Do the Right Thing

One of the most powerful values I acquired from my mom was *rightness*, which she defined as doing what's socially expected. Although Mom would sometimes say that balancing one's own interests with the welfare of others is important, it seemed to me that she always put everyone else first.

I can't count the times Mom told me to "do the right thing because it's expected." "Doing the right thing" meant visiting relatives all the time, calling relatives when I wasn't visiting them, listening to same chit chat over and over again, asking the same questions over and over again, bringing gifts and more gifts . . . and more gifts. And for years I tried, but it seemed the harder I tried, the higher the "right thing" bar was raised. Being there for others consumed so much time that I was constantly behind schedule, and still, the demands increased. My efforts were all out of proportion to whatever good I was able to accomplish. I felt I was never going to be *right* enough. I began to question the value of rightness as Mom defined it.

Do the right thing. I began to resist when I heard those words. I would tearfully ask, *What about me? Why doesn't he call me? Why doesn't anyone else offer to help?* Shocked, my mother would shout back. The conversations about doing the right thing turned into terrible arguments.

I reached the tipping point when I took a job abroad that permitted me only a few vacation weeks in my home country per year. Every day started with the question: "Have you called A, B, C, and D? And what about E? Have you scheduled something with F, G, and H?" My whole visit to my hometown was eaten up with phone calls to my extended family, running from one relative to the next, delivering gifts, and answering the same questions again and again. I had no time to even think of doing things my heart begged for, such as visiting some places where I had created many beautiful childhood memories or have a coffee alone, reflecting on where I started my life journey. When it was time to go back to work, I was exhausted and in need of a real vacation.

When I tried cutting back on the number of visits, Mom was appalled. "How can you not go see them? They've waited for months for you to come home." And, "She's getting older. Who knows how long you'll have a chance to be with her?" And my favorite: "If you don't care enough to go on your own, do it for me. It hurts me that you can't see the right thing to do here."

Finally, I'd had it. But I didn't stop at cutting back on the calls and visits—I refused to be involved in anything connected to my mother's definition of rightness. I didn't call some family members for years.

I didn't really understand why I stopped seeing the people I love until I started researching human values. Through my research, I realized that I had gone through an internal shift: Because *rightness* was no longer a value of mine, I didn't want anything to do with it. I also saw how my internal shift had impacted my relationships. When I realized that I hadn't called my uncle for two years, I felt horrible. My family was the best part of my childhood, and I had many great memories with him. I immediately called for a chat, and before I left town, I went to visit him. When he saw me, his eyes filled with tears. He was really ill. I know it would be hard to forgive myself if I hadn't re-established this relationship before it was too late.

My revelation happened when I framed the situation within my own value system. Rather than viewing my family as an obligation, part of my mother's value system, I began to see them as people I love and appreciate very much. Once I started to act on my own values, I found that I did have the time and energy I needed to see many of these special people nearly every time I went home, while texting and calling them frequently became pleasant, enjoyable, and exciting again.

Although Mom had only the best intentions, she was trying to motivate me from her own perspective of what it means to do the right thing. Now that I'm clear about my own core *and* acquired values, I continue to remind myself of how foolishly we can act when we reject a value.

IF YOU DON'T LIKE THE BATHWATER, TAKE A SHOWER. DON'T THROW OUT THE BABY.

The message I'm trying to communicate is not that we should simply discard our acquired values. Many of them serve us well. Instead, I am encouraging us to fully understand our two sets of values, core and acquired, and then *consciously choose* which to embrace and which to let go. When we accomplish that, we are positioned to succeed.

Insider tip: When you feel you really, really, really *should* achieve/have/be something, instead of rushing into action, take a moment and reflect on other values that will be put on standby if you wholeheartedly pursue that something. Imagine a typical day. Think of the values (and corresponding behaviors) that you'd have to give up. Then and only then, you can choose, day after day, what to do to align your life with what matters the most and reduce the harmful Expectation-Reality Gap. You will experience not just elusive happiness, but true joy and fulfillment.

Thought Experiment: When is Enough, Enough?

- When you think about trying harder and investing more, what is the first thing that comes to mind? Which behaviors would you place before the "set point," and which might occur beyond it?

- When you think about rejecting a value, what is the first thing that comes to mind? As a hint, think of the things that instantly turn you off while interacting with others.

THE BIG TAKEAWAY

I used to think that acquired values only make things complicated, but I've learned that we need these values. Our acquired values are vital for creating relationships and a sense of belonging and for feeling safe in the environment where we live or work. But we also need to know that the values we've acquired from our family, generation, and culture are simply our acquired values, neither good nor bad in and of themselves. They are not the tiniest bit more or less real than other people's familial, generational, or cultural values.

In order to thrive in today's world, we must be able to recognize the filters through which we're watching the world. When we don't, we risk losing track of ourselves and our life's purpose. We make assumptions about how things *should* be, and we take everything unfamiliar as a personal challenge, attack, or insult. We get hurt. We judge others and ourselves. But understanding our acquired values can restore our openness, curiosity, and joy by making judgmental bitterness and negative emotions vanish.

If you can take a bird's eye view of your value system past and present, you will learn to understand and appreciate the differences. You'll be able to make mindful choices that feel right for you. When we offer our best selves to others, we embody a wellbeing whose greater effects reach beyond ourselves and into the world, igniting a chain reaction of happiness.

If you're thinking, "Yeah, all of this sounds great, Senka, but *how do I actually do this?*" you're in luck. In the next section of the book, I'll walk you through the practical steps that will help you transform the knowledge you've just gained into manageable and meaningful changes. Becoming the self you were born to be isn't going to be easy, but it will be simple—I promise.

IV.

Transforming Your World

Chapter 9

Becoming the Self You Were Born to Be

(This is the longest chapter, but that's why you bought the book, right?)

Before we can talk about how to bring more of what we are naturally driven to into our life, we need to work through the process of peeling back the different layers of our acquired values. Why? Because our unexamined acquired values are what holds us back from dedicating ourselves to our core values.

Let's recap: As we strive for positive change, we encounter acquired values that may have been getting in our way for many years. We bring those values from childhood into adulthood as a sort of "carry-on baggage." We've packed our baggage full of the advice, opinions, and beliefs we acquired from the surroundings in which we grew up, nicely folded in the form of life values. Opening the baggage that we've been filling since we were born is not an easy task. It requires disrupting the safe order we've created. Analyzing each compartment of our "luggage" will likely create more of a mess than we currently have, and from that disorderly pile of stuff, we'll need to choose what to keep and what to discard, restoring the unnecessary and broken pieces and reassembling the new structure to accommodate our joy and happiness. Reprogramming our old patterns may take months or even years of effortful thinking and acting because peeling off the layers of our acquired values is—as I've learned in my practice— quite a complex process.

When we decide that we want to improve an aspect of our life, we often look for big changes right away. What we'd really like is a quick fix, something we can get that'll make our lives good and keep them that way. This is understandable because it's the story we have been sold. "Buy this pill and feel better *instantly*. Read this book and feel better *instantly*. Take this class and feel better *instantly*." But those promises are not real; there is no pill, book, or class that will work in the long run if it's not followed by intrinsically-motivated hard work. The hard work required to fight the social forces of our acquired values may be messy and complicated (instead of sexy and glamorous like we might have hoped for). Instead of immediate gratification or quick fixes, we need to embrace change in a systematic way, recognizing that real transformation is likely to be slow and incremental—but it will *last*.

Don't get me wrong—I am not trying to discourage you. I'm 100 percent positive you can make your core values aligned with your three basic psychological needs the center of your life, enjoying all the mental and physical benefits that come with them. I have seen it often enough that I can confidently say that *everyone* can make significant progress and change for the better by understanding their value sets and acting on the inconsistencies within them. And I hope to help by offering the know-how for taming acquired values.

One of the most effective strategies for introducing lasting changes in behavior I've ever encountered is Milton Rokeach's confrontation technique ("hypocrisy"). Rokeach argued that by studying the inconsistencies between our values and our behaviors, we increase our self-awareness. We can then initiate value shifts by facing up to those moments when our actions and values don't align. For example, let's say you value *equality*, but when you take a long hard look at your schedule, you realize you're not engaging in any activity that supports social coherence. You will likely feel some discomfort (you'll feel like a hypocrite) that will either prompt you to action or will help you realize that equality isn't actually a high-priority value of yours.

I like Rokeach's approach. But, like almost every existing coaching exercise about values, he doesn't bring acquired values into the picture. So, I've adapted Rokeach's method for our two different sets of values. We can advance his "value re-education" by understanding that it may be your acquired values causing that uncomfortable, "I'm-a-hypocrite" feeling. If we go back to our example and take into account the role of acquired values, we might understand that you're too preoccupied with your shoulds (your acquired values) to really nurture *equality* in your life. Or, it could be that equality is actually an acquired value, which is repeatedly failing to spark your momentum. This "upgraded" approach relies not only on feeling discomfort, but also on the relief and excitement you'll experience when you catch yourself prioritizing acquired values over core values and when you realize that you can use your awareness to reverse those toxic thoughts and behaviors.

PEEL, DON'T CHOP

I'm about to share with you the twelve steps you'll need to take to align your needs, values, and behaviors to serve you best. This process may sound easy at first, but while it may be a *simple* process, it's not at all *easy*. Here's what I mean: After introducing this strategy to my clients, what I hear most often is a version of, *This makes sense to me, it's logical and simple. How come we humans have so much trouble with something that feels so intuitive?* I remind my clients that it took years of input, internalization, and action on our side to integrate our acquired values into our lives.

For me, the whole process felt exactly like peeling an onion. Some pieces of the skin easily fell off, but some were sticky and persistent. Peeling brought on a few tears and a bitter taste in my mouth. Some of those sticky pieces I intentionally left on, knowing they wouldn't harm my delicious "meal." Plus, I didn't feel guilty for not removing those extra-sticky pieces because I owned the decision to keep them.

Before you jump to the twelve steps, please envision your change as a process, with its ups and downs. *Be gentle on yourself.* Just because something is not easy doesn't mean that it can't be fun, so don't forget to enjoy and celebrate every step on your way to change!

Step #1: Pay Attention

The first step of this process is becoming aware of your acquired values in action. I know this sounds like a no-brainer, but in reality, it can be very complicated. Sometimes, the acquired value at work will be pretty obvious, and you'll recognize it as something acquired from your mom, dad, brother, sister, childhood friend, media, etc. But some messages are so deeply embedded in our brains that it's difficult to accept they are not universal truths. For those deeply imprinted values, the best indicator of an acquired value at work is negative emotions, especially *judgment* toward yourself (*I should do/be/have more*) or others (*they are so unfair/superficial/egoistic/lacking manners*), followed by a creeping feeling in your stomach or other type of bodily tension.

Such negative emotions or tensions occur when our acquired values are activated. They try to switch us into default mode—the well-worn neural path. When we try to resist even for a very short moment, the angry little Chihuahua from Chapter 3 feels threatened, and it will bark at us, reminding us of how things *should* be. And if things aren't as they *should* be, then either we are failing or others around us are failing. We experience unpleasant thoughts or bodily sensations that send us spiraling down into more judgment. The more judgment, the more we distance ourselves from others and the more we believe we're not good enough. And in the long run, this can snowball into real threats to our wellbeing.

Once I made the connection between negative emotions and acquired values, I felt like I'd discovered the key to a door that had been locked for a long time. I could finally understand and recognize my acquired value of *unity* for what it was—my acquired value. And it helped me contextualize all the crappy things I'd felt when I first moved to Austria.

I felt like I had won a triple jackpot when I got accepted into the PhD program in experimental cardiology at the Medical University of Graz. At the competitive selection process (two-day onsite interview), I was a total outsider, presenting the work I'd done in a country that, at the time, struggled to repair its basic infrastructure after twenty years of war. Because of my work under challenging circumstances, acceptance in the program meant even more to me. I couldn't wait to move to my new city and, most importantly for my Serbian soul, meet the members of the research team and create some meaningful connections.

But instead of the friendship and connections I longed for, I got an important lesson.

In a state of absolute excitement, as soon as I arranged my 280-square-foot studio apartment, I invited the entire team for a coffee-and-cake-get-to-know-each-other-afternoon at my place. Despite my efforts to keep the atmosphere cozy, I sensed that my lab mates felt awkward. I could see that they found it strange I had tried to squeeze so many people into such a small apartment—the happy spirit I was used to was nowhere in sight. They were polite, but distant. No one ever mentioned gathering again. They politely rejected the next invitation with all sort of excuses. And I haven't received any invitations for a long time.

The feeling of rejection and loneliness was difficult to digest. I went from feeling on the top of the world (when I got the position) to feeling desperate (when I failed to make friends) in a very short time. Although I managed to stay positive for most of the time, in my darker moments, I questioned my decision to move; I questioned my character, myself in general, but also my new co-workers and their moral compass. *Why am I even here*, I wondered.

Today, after several years and many ups and downs, I can recognize that the way I felt in that moment—the loneliness, confusion, disappointment and rejection—is the definition of acquired values at work. And, as I've already mentioned, my acquired value of *unity* tends not to go over too well with the people raised to be reserved around me.

So, how can we avoid the shame-and-blame spirals of negative emotions and judgment?

The first step in your new thinking pattern is simply allowing yourself to notice your conflicts and bring your inner battles into your full awareness. Pay attention when you start judging. You don't need to explain, interpret, or analyze your emotions here. Just be aware of them. Nothing more, nothing less. For those extra-deep acquired values, you will most likely have to experience negative emotions several times before you finally understand what's happening (like me, after my fiasco party). So be persistent, pay attention even to the situations where you are *very sure* it's just "how things should be."

Step #2: Give Yourself Space

We face the decision of which value to respond to several hundred times every day. Should I go to the gym (appearance) or spend a pleasant afternoon with my partner (joy)? Should a let my crying baby sooth itself (strength), or should I keep rocking him till he stops (dedication)? Should I text back my partner who has hurt my feelings (loyalty) or pretend I haven't read his text (dominance)? Should I express my negative feelings toward my mother-in-law (honesty) or should I keep them to myself (respect)?

The loud, nagging voice of our strongest acquired values is so attention-grabbing that, most of the time, we don't feel as if we even have a choice. We feel pressured into whatever our acquired value and its persuasive advocate (woof woof) suggests we need to do; otherwise, we think, we'll face negative consequences. The key in taming this voice is to increase the bubble between external input that requires a decision and our reaction to it. I call this gap between the stimulus and our reaction the *awareness space*.[72] Think of it like social distancing for your values: the larger the space, the more conscious choices you can make.

Here's how to increase your awareness space. When an event triggers your acquired values, you:

- Pause and notice your negative emotions
- Notice that your acquired values are activated
- Ask yourself, "What choices do I have in this situation?"

Bam! With those pauses to notice what's going on with you emotionally and by looking for a choice instead of an obligation, you've just increased your "awareness space."

Step #3: Be Prepared

To recognize your acquired values and where they come from, it's super important to choose a stimulating strategy for reflection that works for you. Ask yourself in advance: *When I notice that I'm getting really upset next time, how am I going to reflect on the values involved?* You can choose to reflect alone, or

---

72 Although I recognized this bubble of space from my own experience long before I engaged in the coaching program, later I read about the similar concept under different names (e.g. "choice points" by Susan David, PhD, or "cognitive control" by Daniel Goleman, PhD), which further strengthen my belief that this space is a key for changing your behavior.

you may decide to get some help along the way. If you prefer working on your own, and you know you have consistency when it comes to controlling your mental behavior and persisting even when you feel tired and life is complicated, I encourage you to do so. If you don't know if you can do it on your own, here are two things to consider: your environment and anticipating obstacles.

Sugar? Free!

Several months before writing this chapter, I decided not to consume anything that has added sugars in it. I knew it would be tough, but it has been *much* tougher than I thought it would be. More difficult than not eating sweets was explaining to every single person at work, at conferences, at children's birthday parties, or at friend's dinners or gatherings that I don't eat sugars because I had traces of glucose in my urine during my second pregnancy. I completely misjudged my environment and their (not that supportive) reactions, "Oh, you're so weird" or "Take everything away from me but leave me my chocolate." I actually expected more support because at the end of the day, this is a decision that most people consider a healthy one.

I was lucky to face only one real obstacle: lunch at my in-law's place, where my mother-in-law routinely makes donuts (an Austrian version, *Krapfen*) especially for me because she knows they are my all-time favorites. But I felt conflicted about telling her about my decision with sugar. I didn't want to offend her or appear ungrateful for her special effort. As you see, real obstacles are the situations, which involve the people you deeply care about. In this moment, I faced a choice: either go against my value of *respect* or go against my values of *integrity* and *commitment* to what I think is best for me.

So, what do you think I did? Well, I'm not going to tell you. Instead, I'll give you this thought experiment: What would *you* choose, dear reader—to eat the donut or leave it? Consider this thought experiment as a way to test your own values!

Step # 4: Secure Your Support Community

My dear introverted friends, you are free to skip this step. I fully believe that those who want to, can go through this process on their own. For many of us, though, navigating the rocky terrain of our acquired values is easier with the loving support of others. Teaming up transforms a personal quest into a shared one (reinforcing our basic psychological need for bonding and connection). Hence, nothing sustains motivation better than finding your team. That's why I highly encourage you to consider one of the three "team-based" strategies.

Option One: The Breakfast Club

Find a buddy with the same goal (i.e. to decode the values that are in play when you become judgmental or upset) to team up with. This can be your partner, friend, or a family member. As a team, make a commitment to follow through and keep each other accountable for reflection and expanding self-awareness. Or, in an ideal case, see whether your entire family wants to engage in changing a specific value-behavior pattern(s) together. Keep in mind that your current standing won't determine how successful you'll be as team.

Long before I was aware of core and acquired values, I was part of a not-dream and un-likely-to-happen team. It was the year 2007, and I had six (most difficult) exams to complete my studies in biochemistry. Prior to that, I had left my university for a year due to personal and family struggles. When I solemnly declared to my Mom that I'd finish my degree in the next six months, she laughed. She didn't think I had the slightest chance. On that Sunday evening, I decided to take one last stroll through the city before locking myself in my room to study, leaving only when I needed to take an exam. While walking and pondering on how nobody believed it was possible, I met a friend who seemed weirdly overexcited about my six-month plan. *What's with her*, I thought.

I soon learned that Jane also needed an academic Plan B. When she found out she was pregnant, she had rushed into marriage with her high school sweetheart, mainly because of family pressure, even though both Jane and her boyfriend weren't too excited about the relationship anymore. She lost the baby but still had a nightmare dream wedding (a.k.a. her mother-in-law's dream wedding). When I met Jane, she was suffering from something my Mom calls post-wedding depression. "You're my light at the end of the tunnel. Please let me join you, and we'll study those six months together; I need something positive happening in my life," she said.

"Glad to have you on board," I said. And I meant it more than she could possibly imagine.

When she called me later that evening, I thought she was giving up. But Jane had met another colleague of ours, Kiara, with whom I had had a major fight during the first semester and hadn't talked to ever since. Kiara asked to join the "desperate student" club after her supposed-to-be-forever-love broke up with her, revealing he'd been dating another girl—whom he now planned to marry. Considering our history, I came to the conclusion that Kiara must feel really messed up if she's asking to spend days and days with me. So, she was instantly granted membership into this weird, unlikely trio, consisting of borderline anorexic Kiara, marriage-depressed Jane, and the accidental utopist regisseur, "The Return of the Written Offs," a.k.a.—me.

Fast-forward six months from the first "study date." We celebrated passing our last exam, I scored 10/10 on all six exams, finishing as the best student in class, while both Kiara and Jane scored way above their averages over the past five years. Although finishing our studies was important, even more important was the lesson to never (ever) underestimate the power of teaming up. It has been thirteen years since these circumstances brought an unlikely trio together and, guess what, we're still friends. In fact, both of them became part of my "inner circle" of real friends. Although I sure appreciate my story's happy ending, I share this with you to emphasize the point that when you join forces around something important, you tend to form lasting connections. *Cue the Simple Minds' "Don't You (Forget About Me)."*[73]

Option Two: Yes, Coach

Connect with a coach who will keep you accountable and help you implement the "external voice recognition software" to your daily thinking and decision-making. Don't be afraid to ask for help with this. I wish I'd had a coach around for my battle with my national/cultural value of unity and my lab mates, instead of being hurt for years. No friend or family member could really relate to the situation. Serbian friends whole-heartedly rooted for unity as the right way,

---

73 Simple Minds. "Don't You (Forget About Me)" from the film *The Breakfast Club*. A&M Records, 1985.

calling Austrians cold and distanced. Austrian friends felt uncomfortable with *too much* opening up, thinking Serbs are weak and lack manners for invading their privacy. A good coach, I believe, could've helped me diagnose my problem in no time. (Friendly Tip: If you opt for a coach, check www.science2wellbeing. com for one specialized in values.)

Option Three: Get Involved

Consider joining a club or a community likely to attract people in similar situations to yours. Such discussions may help you reflect on your values or how you can diminish the negative effects of some of your acquired values. Humans crave bonding and connection. That's why when you join a book or sport club, an amateur band, climate change movement, new moms' community, or post-burnout support group, you may more easily find like-minded people and may feel more comfortable to openly discuss intimate topics.

No matter which option you decide is right for you, it's important to have your strategy ready. Know what you will do or to whom you'll turn when the wind of judgment starts blowing.

Step #5: Keep Digging

When the battle for the "value throne" begins, negative emotions flood our minds and soon our bodies, as well. Only this time you know what's going on. Now, your biggest but most difficult task is to listen carefully and figure out from where this voice originates.

In honor of my friend, Jenni, who was obsessed with Indiana Jones as a kid, I'm going to use an archaeological metaphor. Think of your acquired values as hidden treasures (or fossils if *practicality* is a core value of yours), buried deep beneath layers and layers of earth. You are the archeologist in charge of unearthing these precious artifacts. To reach your object, you could use a jackhammer and backhoe, blasting and scooping your way into the soil. But because you're going full force, you might miss your artifacts or damage them in the process. Instead, you'll need your whole toolbox of delicate archeological tools, from small hammers and shovels to brushes for carefully brushing away the dirt. And patience. You'll need to keep chipping away, going slowly so you don't miss or damage anything. You see where I'm going?

Like those buried artifacts, our acquired values are programmed deep within us, and locating the one we want to bring to the surface requires patience. Instead of trowels or brushes, we use a series of questions and self-reflections to slowly identify which acquired value is the cause of our negative emotions.

Since we are all different, and we all have different acquired values, I can't give you a "one size fits all" map, with an *X* to mark the spot of your acquired values. I can only encourage you to dig deeper and deeper, until you hit the one word that rings true for you, and you'll say, "*Yes*. That's it."

Be Modest!

Here's an example from my client Peter. Peter was eager to discover his acquired values. He'd come to each coaching session with a list of situations and people that triggered his judgmental thinking. In one session, he explained how his colleague constantly irritated him.

"What was upsetting about her?" I asked.

"Everything," he laughed. "I mean, professionally she's OK, but this image of how she's presenting herself is so annoying."

"How is she presenting herself?"

"Like not being busy but having an awesome lifestyle, lots and lots of money, and being very liberal."

"What's annoying about that?"

"Well, she's so superficial—one of those irritating San Francisco hipster stereotypes."

"How *should* she be?"

"I don't know. But definitely not the San Francisco hipster smart aleck."

"You know I'm not from the area; what's so annoying about San Francisco hipsters?"

"They pretend they are better than they are."

"What do you mean by that?"

"Well, they present themselves as having it all sorted out. Like they are so great. They brag about their awesomeness, while believing all the others have gotten it all wrong."

"But you think they are not great?"

"Well, not really."

"What makes one great?"

"Knowledge. Mastery. Intelligence. And originality."

"And those that are not super-intelligent, knowledgeable masters with world-changing ideas, how *should* they be?"

"They *should* be modest. They should be f***ing modest."

From his tone and body language and the high levels of judgment in his choice of words, it was instantly clear to me that *modesty* is one of Peter's top acquired values. Still, Peter needed to hear himself boiling all his judgments down to *modesty* before he was able to let go of "this is how people should be" and reconsider his beliefs around modesty. We eventually reached his buried belief that not anyone without a Nobel Prize, prestigious national research funding—or at least 100 peer-reviewed publications in top scientific journals—should act as if they've done something big in life. They should especially *not* have their own blogs/channels/websites, which was also the main reason he didn't have a proper marketing scheme for his own business . . .

Although every person struggles with different acquired values, the really good news about understanding those values is that we only have a couple of very strong ones. In my experience with a three-digit number of clients, usually one to three acquired values are strong, dominant, and it's these three which are involved in 90 percent of our judgments, conflicts, or hurtful situations. So, basically every second or every third situation in which you notice your acquired values at work will, if you dig deep enough, come down to the same thing. Cheers to that!

Step #6: Know the Difference

Clea is a client who explained that she acquired the value *tolerance* because her grandfather was a Nazi. Her family was careful to teach her that her grandfather's choices are the darkest spot in their family history and that *tolerance,* under any circumstance, is absolutely crucial. As we discussed the concept of core versus acquired values, I could see how much she struggled with labeling acquired values as something negative. For my Clea and all other Cleas out there who like some of their acquired values, I will repeat once again: not all acquired values are bad. In the case of my Clea, the value of *tolerance* had two aspects: the core *and* the acquired one.

When the external voices of our acquired values are aligned with our core values, we can experience our acquired values in positive, non-toxic ways. Thus, it's important to know the difference between a benign or positive acquired value and a toxic, harmful one. If pursuing your acquired value feels comfortable, if it doesn't drain a lot of your energy or make you change the course of your life toward something you don't really want at the cost of something you do, this value isn't likely to be toxic. If you like your acquired value, and it feels good for you to choose it, go on and embrace it. Just be mindful of avoiding judgment toward others who don't appreciate the value as much as you do. For example, Clea could change her attitude about others who express less *tolerance* by understanding that her special environment put an inflated focus on this value, and others may not have had a similar upbringing.

After his coaching, Peter decided to hold onto the aspects of *modesty* that enriched his life while consciously choosing not to weaponize this value by judging others. I still choose the value of *unity* in its same exaggerated form, even though I know it is a learned one. I'll always try to make connections by offering *unity* because I believe in its positive qualities. But now, I accept when others aren't interested in or willing to accept my offer, and I no longer feel rejected or hurt. Knowing the difference between toxic and non-toxic forms of our acquired values allows us to mindfully hold on to the values that serve us. But for those acquired values that feel like a burden, it's time to say good-bye.

Step #7: Rewind the Tape

Once you've identified the acquired value that keeps toggling your judgmental mode to *on*, you'll want to decide if this value is poisoning your life with toxic energy. In my coaching, I encourage people to start by "rewinding the movie" of their lives back to the time when they internalized the value in question. This helps you understand the "big picture" of the role your acquired values have played in your life.

To help you time travel back to the moment when you acquired this value, give your most honest answer to these three questions:

- What is my precise definition of this value?
- What is my most honest belief about this value?
- From whom did I get this value and this belief? When? How?

Take your time with the last question. Notice the first thought that comes to mind when you consider this belief. What situations have contributed to your holding this belief? Think of the specific words or phrases you remember about this value and your belief behind it.

When trying to understand my acquired value *success*, I focused on defining what *success* really means to me. I figured that my definition would be very simple: *Success* is winning. When you win, you are successful; when you don't win, you are a loser. To answer the next question, I defined my belief like this: *To have a good life, you have to be successful.* When I combined those beliefs, I saw the code for success that my brain had programmed in: *To have a good life you have to keep winning.* Reflecting on how I acquired this value in the form I have just described, the first thing that came to mind was winning the drawing competition, the situation I told you about in Chapter 3. Although it was more than thirty years ago, I vividly remember the attention I received from my microenvironment, my kindergarten friends, and teachers. I had never had so much attention up to that point in life. I also remembered how for my tenth birthday, my family gave me a tea mug with a funny cartoon of Foghorn Leghorn saying, "If you want to win you must not lose" (not all that funny in the context of my life, ha?). As I grew up, I continued to receive attention and praise for winning things, reinforcing my kindergarten self's observation that winning will bring me the greatest satisfaction and appreciation in life.

I asked myself whether or not I really, truly believe that constant winning is what makes for a good life. When I was honest with myself, I realized that I actually don't believe that at all. Instead, failing has played a huge part in shaping my character—in a mostly positive way. I learned so many important lessons from the times I've failed, and I honestly don't believe I would have been able to achieve many things in my life without those lessons.

I decided to let go of this belief and instead create a new one—one I willingly choose and that makes sense and feels true for me. *Success is having your three basic needs satisfied as much as possible under the circumstances you are currently in* feels much better to me. To be frank, I added the last part of this belief when I became a mom. It made me realize there are specific situations in life when you can't quite balance all of your three needs the way you want, despite your most sincere intent and dedication.

Step # 8: Zoom Out to Zoom In

Once you can visualize how you acquired this value, try to watch the movie of your life since you adopted this value. Can you "zoom out" from your life to see the bigger picture? Think of the most important decisions you've made based on your pursuit of this value. How did those situations turn out for you? Have you possibly chosen a career you don't particularly like? Have you chosen a partner who is not quite a match just because they fit your ideal look, education, origin, religion, age, or a combination of those? Have you devoted your free time to the activities that fulfill the American dream but not *your* dream? How many of these decisions made you content, filled with motivation, and happy to be you? If you could do it all over again, would you stick to those decisions and values? Does this value feel more like a virus, depleting you of the time and energy you need to engage with what really lights up your intrinsic motivation?

This visualization technique will provide a clearer picture on the "life" of this acquired value, from your young self who received the information and internalized the message to your aging self, continuously choosing this value when making important decisions, without questioning whether you're following your own or someone else's vision of what you should do to be fulfilled, successful, loved, or cared for. It may sound like a contradiction, but "zooming out" on the life of an acquired value actually helps you "zoom in" on which of your acquired values have served you and which have undermined you (please ask your buddy, coach, or community for help if you get stuck).

Sebastian's Story

I worked with a client who identified *"winners make progress, losers make excuses"* as the advice he heard the most from his parents. As a young boy, Sebastian interpreted this to mean that he should advance at work by climbing the corporate ladder, from the very bottom to the very top. He started in a low position in a company and strived wholeheartedly to become the head of his department one day. He placed so much value on the promotion that when the call for the position was announced, and he felt ready to go for it, he neglected every other area of his life to focus completely on the selection. He worked day and night to increase his chances of getting the position; after all, he'd be the loser if he didn't succeed. He was on the edge of burning out and on the edge of getting a divorce.

Re-evaluating his acquired values and associated beliefs was an eye-opener for Sebastian. The belief he wrote was: "If I am not on the very top, I am a loser." I still remember his surprise when he looked at the sentence he wrote, and when I told him that I don't believe it's true: "Not only do I believe it's untrue, but probably at least 80 percent of the population doesn't believe this. Ask your wife, for example." He was sincerely shocked. Until that moment, he had never ever questioned the validity of this belief.

"Wow," he realized, "this actually means I don't need to become the head of the department to be successful? I definitely need time to process this!"

That was the only thing he was able to say before he asked to terminate the session.

Step # 9: "Let it Go"[74]

Step nine is all about finally choosing to *distance* yourself from the values that no longer serve you. The process of value re-evaluation is particularly important for values created through small social traumas. When you understand how the acute value formation happened, you can critically review the situation and decide if this value still holds true for you or not. Am I a stupid cow, or was my teacher only frustrated with me for not following her instructions? Does the woman really have to eat poo in the relationship, or was that something my mom

---

74   Idina Menzel. "Let It Go" from the film the Disney's *Frozen*. 2013.

told me based on her own experiences and misery? When you can "re-view" a painful situation you have been suppressing for a long, long time, you may, in fact, immediately see that what happened was not your fault. And, furthermore, you are free to discard the harmful belief.

A friend of mine has an apt metaphor for the act of discarding the harmful beliefs we've internalized from external sources. She says, "When someone—and sometimes that 'someone' is yourself—tries to hand over toxic ideas or emotions, wrapped up as acquired values with bright red ribbons of guilt, shame, and negativity—simply refuse the package."

Oh, hi voice. It's you again. My dad sent you, eh? Well, I have to disappoint you today. Today, I'm choosing not to accept the package. Return to sender!

So, put on that shiny blue dress (literally or figuratively—your choice), bring out your best inner-Elsa, and "let it go."

Step #10: Train Your Brain

It's hard to recognize and change life-long thought patterns and roles. But with conscious and consistent effort—and patience—*you will* do it. Now that you've mastered the crucial step of recognizing your behavioral patterns and understanding which values and beliefs drive them, you're ready to take the next step in your positive change journey. To create new patterns, you will have to actively let go the old ones many times before the new ones become automatic. But the good news is that scientists have discovered that our brain has a capacity to actually rewire itself.

Thought patterns create neural pathways that act like ruts in a well-traveled road. When faced with a decision, we default to the well-worn path. And trying to change a default pattern by simply not acting on it actually makes it stronger and more resistant—"what you resist persists," as the saying goes. But when we combine new thoughts with new actions, our old neuronal pathways shrivel from lack of use, and, eventually, our new thoughts and behaviors become the default. We can literally override our brains and create changes on the neurological level.

We scientists call this unique trait "brain plasticity." Our brain's plasticity means that our brains aren't reaching their final maturity in early life and decaying from there as we age; they continue to produce new cells and synapsis all life long. In fact, we generate a great number of new neurons in the dentate gyrus of the hippocampus, a brain region necessary for various processes of learning. The lesser-known fact, however, is that most of our brain's restocked cells die off within weeks.[75] What prevents neuronal death and helps them successfully "integrate" in the existing neuronal network is involvement in so-called "effortful" learning process.

So what is it about learning that keeps new neurons alive? Very generally, it appears to be the effort involved in learning. Being conscious about your choices is an example of an "effortful" task. The most effective way to put effortful learning in practice and reduce the influence of acquired values is a strategy I like to call "Defaulting versus Conscious Choosing," and it looks like this: To find out if you're working in default mode or consciously choosing a behavior or belief, ask yourself, *Am I acting on a belief I've consciously chosen, or am I defaulting to an old acquired belief?*

To help answer this question, I encourage my clients to create their Values Evaluation Matrix (see my example below) as an effective tool for rewiring the brain. It is a simple three-column table in which you will write the troubling value, the associated belief and, if you're willingly choosing, the new belief you want to program into your brain.

Acquired Value	Old Belief	Chosen Belief
Success	*Success is winning.*	*Success is having your three basic needs satisfied as much as possible under the circumstances you are currently in.*
Your example		

Creating a Values Evaluation Matrix will give you something tangible to turn to when faced with difficult feelings. It will instantly give you a solution,

---

75 Shors, Tracey J. "The Adult Brain Makes New Neurons, and Effortful Learning Keeps Them Alive." *Current Directions in Psychological Science*, 2014.

without spending too much time reflecting on the situation. This one sentence outlining your old belief will instantly remind you how and where you acquired this value, and it will tell you again: It's not an absolute truth and it's not your fault that you used to believe in this. The truly powerful part, however, is having your new belief on hand. Remember, thinking that you don't want to believe something will only reinforce its influence on you. In contrast, calling upon and thinking about a new belief will create and strengthen a new neuronal pattern, slowly changing it to your default mode. You are, essentially, training your brain to respond in a way that leads to better outcomes for you.

Again, you may think this is a no-brainer. But more nuances to come:

When you identify an acquired value created by a small social trauma that's detrimental to your wellbeing, it may be easier to choose new, supportive beliefs and actions. However, if your acquired value was not so obviously "bad" for you, the choice may be much more difficult. For example, consider my value of *success* = *winning*. There was nothing in that equation that made me *directly* feel bad. My situation was complicated because my acquired value of winning was socially appreciated and rewarded, meaning it gave me temporary positive feedback. It actually felt good in the winning moment. The problem was more indirect: I placed too much value on winning, and so I depleted myself of the time and energy I needed to nurture other important areas of my life. Actively choosing to focus less on winning was very difficult because I knew I was giving up on positive feedback and admiration from my surroundings that gave me an intense spike of satisfaction and a temporary boost in self-confidence.

So, when dealing with values that are socially appreciated, you will always feel a certain amount of loss in saying no to things. Giving up the well-worn and familiar path may cause discomfort, and you may be revisiting your decision while feeling sad or guilty every time you think of it. This is how I initially felt when I knew I could have won something but chose not to do it because the price was too high for the other important areas of my life. I knew why I was choosing to do (or not do) something, and I still felt some grief and sadness around it.

However, I learned that when we consciously choose to give up something for a long period of time, and we know *why* we're doing it, we ignite our intrinsic motivation, which helps us navigate cloudy feelings. We can be at peace with our choices, knowing our efforts are creating new neural pathways, training our brains to serve our ultimate wellbeing.

Step #11: A Little Goes a Long Way[76]

When you've set your reflection strategy in place and printed several copies of your Evaluation Matrix to keep on hand (one tacked up in the office, one in the glove box of the car, one on the fridge with a tacky tourist magnet), please remember: nature favors evolution not revolution. Although traditional self-help made promises that raised our expectations to "lofty goals and total transformation," research takes the opposing standpoint. Small, deliberate twists, infused with your values and multiplied by months or years, creates the most dramatic and lasting change.[77]

Each little tweak may not look like much on its own, but the cumulative effect over time is astounding. Imagine, for example, a plane that is flying from Boston, USA to Lisbon, Portugal. If the pilot makes a tiny shift of a few degrees on the flight plan before the plane takes off, it can dramatically change where the plane will end up. Instead of in Europe, you may find yourself arriving in Morocco, on the coast of North Africa! Small changes accrued over time will slowly but surely switch off your default mode and send you someplace different.

The only way we can really be sure the changes we make last is by actively choosing the belief we want, over and over again, until it becomes a new default mode of thinking. I can't tell you how many times you'll need to make a deliberate effort because that number will vary for each individual person, but the moment *will* come when your intentional mode of thinking will reside so deeply in your brain that you'll no longer have to be "intentional" about it. When this happens, your intentional mode of thinking will persist over time with almost no further effort, on good and bad days, whether you are paying attention or not.

---

76 When I was working on the "value study," I read the book *Emotional Agility* by Susan David, PhD. Not only did this book made a huge impact on me personally, but it also articulated many of the strategies I intuitively incorporated in my coaching methodology. I found inspiration for the metaphor of the plane that is flying from Boston to Lisbon and the lofty goals and tiny tweaks in her book, and I use them here with the author's permission.

77 Susan David, PhD. *Emotional Agility*. London: Penguin Life, 2016.

Let me share one really good tip I wish someone had given me long ago: decide in advance what exactly you will do as a replacement for the old, default behavior when pressured by your acquired values and all the external and internal *shoulds*. Think of it as a corresponding behavior to your chosen belief. For example, when I think of my acquired value of success, my old, defaulting behavior would be to completely neglect all other aspects of my life and have a laser-sharp focus on what has to be done to win. Today, I choose to revisit my "apple tree" and assess how much damage will be done to my other basic psychological needs, and my wellbeing as a whole, before I go for a challenge.

The key to your success will be to set a *doable* behavior that won't require a huge effort all at once. An easy example: I decided not to eat sweets, so what do I do with those inevitable chocolate cravings? Or when my whole family eats ice cream? Because I *knew* I'd crave chocolate, I needed an alternative to chocolate, one that would still feel good. If I set a strategy that's unrealistic and difficult, like doing twenty squats every time I think of chocolate, I'd probably give up on the same day. But if I made a thoroughly-planned, stretch strategy, I could increase my chances tremendously. I decided to drink one cup of sugar-free oat or almond milk every time I would normally eat sweets. I chose oat or almond milk after I considered which tastes I enjoy the most (I love the taste of plant-based milk), and how much sugars are present in each serving (even if I drink it five times a day, I'm still adding 0g of sugar to my count). Instead thinking what I *should* do or telling myself *no, no, no* in moments of crisis, I calmly walk to my fridge and pour a cup of milk. And now that I've been doing this for many months, I can tell you that I find myself needing my sugar-replacement-plant-based-milk less and less, except on stressful days. Think of it this way: When you know what exactly

you'll choose to do instead of your toxic default action response, you'll already have done half of the work.

By choosing the new way of thinking and behaving more often, over time, it will inevitably become the well-worn path. The nagging little Chihuahua will slowly start feeling comfortable in the new environment and won't be afraid of the unknown anymore. It will become supportive of the consciously chosen path. And just imagine how much easier life will be when your unflappable Chihuahua tells you that what you *should* do is the same thing that you actually *want* to do.

My recommendation: Don't quit all activities related to your acquired values (or your job!) or make any sudden, drastic changes in your life. I'd love to see you become conscious of the ways your core and acquired values influence your thinking and behavior, and then use this new awareness to actively reorganize your value system to serve you best, by changing your thinking and acting habits, bit by bit. Over time, the cumulative effects of a number of small changes will spontaneously bring about significant positive change in your life.

Step #12: Know Your Core Values

Now that you've removed some of the roadblocks and are ready for more of the good stuff, the time to think about your core values has finally arrived.

How do you satisfy your need for autonomy, relatedness, and competence? Here are three big ideas to think about.

Your Perfect Month

When trying to figure out what you truly need to feel *autonomous*, try thinking about what you *would choose* to do in your free time, if you could really do anything you want. No money issues, no time issues, best possible care for your children is provided, you've just successfully finished a huge and meaningful campaign at work (your boss insists you'll get paid leave for the next month), and your partner is busy with a huge deadline to meet (so, you're completely on your own). You have all the time and resources for yourself.

Skip the thought that you will sleep for the first seventy-two hours or just stay in bed watching Netflix and enjoying your favorite food and drinks delivered to you. Think further, past those three days. Now, you are fresh and energized, and you can do absolutely anything. What would you *choose* to do? Would you read and learn? Meditate? Plant an apple orchard? Would you invite friends for a camping trip? Take a cooking class? Would you paint? Do pottery? Go bungee jumping?

When we are free to choose with no boundaries, we choose the things that really resonate with our souls and give us a sense of freedom. And we always choose the same *type* of activity that is rooted in our core values. You may act on your sense of *creativity, adventure, humor, personal-growth, persistence, dedication, relaxing, reflecting, awareness* or . . . you name it.

For me, my perfect month would be devoted to reflection, personal-growth, and awareness.

I asked a friend of mine who teaches literature at a university what she would do during her perfect month. I imagined her in a cozy reading chair, reading stacks and stacks of book. She surprised me when she told me that she'd spend her "me-time" stripping and painting furniture, making bookshelves, redoing the decorations on her walls, and putting together a new "look" for her bedroom with new linens and decorations. And she'd clean her house from top to bottom and then plan a Mediterranean vacation to visit her best friend in Cyrpus. Sure, there'd be plenty of book reading, but, with all the time and resources in the world, my friend would pursue her core values of *productivity, art/creativity/design,* and *travel/adventure/fun* while fulfilling her basic needs.

Your Best Relationships

Let's take a look at the values that structure your most meaningful relationships. Think of the three best relationships with others that you have. What specifically makes them better than the rest? Deep intimate conversations? Lots of fun and laughter together? Genuineness and honesty? Longevity? Ability to be fully open, be yourself? Devotedness and care for each other? Or simplicity and modesty?

If you reflect on your deep versus more superficial relationships hard enough, you will be able to identify characteristics that all of your best relationships have in common. You will also identify the missing pieces in the relationships where you don't feel invested.

For my friend, Dimitri, the three things that his best relationships share are loyalty, compassion, and generosity. His most meaningful relationships are with people who have proved, over time, that they will always have his back, in good times and bad times. They are people who show compassion to themselves, to him, and to others—they have some kind of vision of a kinder, more loving world, and they work to bring that world into existence in some way. Finally, he bonds best with people who show generosity and give freely and lovingly because this is also how he shows his care. His friends know that if they pick up the check this time, he'll get the next one, and vice versa. He feels totally comfortable going to his closest friends when he needs help, and they know his Zoom window is always open.

Lead the Way, Minister of . . .

And finally, to learn about the values that give you a sense of competence and a feeling that you contribute to the welfare of others, imagine humanity has created one government for the whole world, and you're about to become a minister in this government. In this government, ministers are not chosen based on their formal education but on their passions and willingness to contribute to specific causes. The government recognizes the biological fact that we humans are naturally driven to help and improve specific causes. That doesn't mean we don't care about other causes; we just feel more passionate and driven when it comes to one or two. When we donate time and energy to one of our specific missions, we feel a sense of purpose. Working feels effortless. This means you could choose to be minister of anything you want.

Which resources would you choose to lead? Youth and education? Health, wellbeing, and social care? Justice? Foreign affairs? Culture? Sports? Science and technology? Environmental protection? Economy?

I would choose Knowledge, Learning, Innovation, Motivation, Inspiration, and Teaching . . . (basically I'd be the minister of Know L.I.M.I.T.)

	autonomy	competence	relatedness
behaviors			
values			
needs	autonomy	competence	relatedness

My professor friend? She's chosen to be the minister of Words, Beaches, and Baby Animals, with a joint role as Assistant Minister of Social Equality & Inclusion.

Don't be afraid to have fun with this exercise—just draw your own "tree of life" on the previous page.

Look at you . . . you just wrote your own unique formula for leading a fulfilled life. I hope you will use it to help you see the bigger picture—as a re-calibration tool and as a guiding principle to actively navigate the rest of your life.

OPPORTUNITIES, BIG AND SMALL

Now that you have the tools to identify and evaluate both sets of your values, you will be able to spot the opportunities related to what matters most to you, and you'll be able to actively pursue those opportunities.

The easiest and most manageable way to accomplish this is by finding small opportunities within your existing, day-to-day actions. Is there a way for you to reframe or adjust your approach to an existing routine that would shift the emphasis from an acquired value to a core value? Can you give more focus and attention to the actions and behaviors that reflect your core values by making a small change?

Over time, as aligning your actions with your core values becomes easier, you might find yourself ready to make larger changes to your life. Do you want to change careers? Find better communication with your loved ones? Discover what roles our acquired and core values play in your parenting skills? We'll talk more about how to find big opportunities and align your career and personal relationships with your core values in the following chapters. Stay calm and carry on, my reader friend.

Chapter 10

Transform Your Close Relationships

We don't function fully without relationships, and on this point, there is a remarkable convergence among social scientists. We know this. Yet, instead of bringing us joy and thriving, our relationships often suffer and our deepest fears and worries, rooted in our acquired values are often to blame. The persistently active, little Chihuahua just won't let go; it fights hard to preoccupy us with our "shoulds," often making us lose sight of what's most important. We become more stubborn about our own beliefs and less empathic toward other peoples'. If we lack awareness about our two value systems and how they show up in our lives, we may easily run into relationship trouble and pull away from those we love most.

HAPPY EVER AFTER?

I think I was still a teenager when I read about marriage statistics for the first time. We've all heard that more than 50 percent of modern marriages end in divorce. What saddens me more, however, is a lesser-known statistic: around an astounding 85 percent of marriages are joyless and could be labeled as dysfunctional. I instantly wanted to know what couples who stay *happily* together do differently than those who don't. Out of my youthful and somewhat naïve curiosity, I asked married people about their strategies for keeping their marriages working in the long run. I was literally speechless to learn that most people haven't even thought about this.

Years later, as a part of my research, I undertook a survey with more than 1,000 twenty- to forty-year-olds, freshly married or engaged participants from all over the world. The survey had only one question:

> *Knowing that 50% of marriages end up with a divorce (and 85% are dysfunctional), what is your strategy for preventing your marriage from failing?*

I offered four answers (the order of answers was randomized) based on things I would repeatedly hear in my "preliminary research" with people I knew:

1. *We love each other—it won't happen to us*
2. *I'll take a chance (15 percent of marriages are happy)*
3. *I haven't thought about it at all*
4. *I have a clear plan of what to do to succeed*

And this was the result.

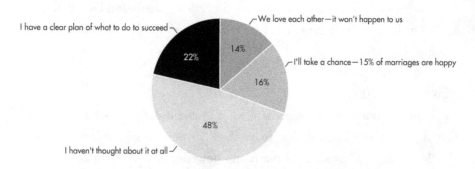

Only a little above twenty percent actively thought of *something* they should do in order to make their marriages last, which is a real surprise as statistics argue that a permanent parting of ways should be a very real concern for most couples. While we routinely consider "investing" in money, education, career, and even hobbies, we rarely reflect on the time and knowledge investment needed to learn how to maintain successful marriages. Why do we think we don't need any skills or knowledge when going into relationships or marriage?

We think of loving relationships as innate to human nature. Things that should come natural to us. If that were true, we would live in alignment with our core values and also choose partners whose core values we fully respect. Instead, we accumulate many layers of acquired values that, when unexamined, mess up the whole story. When we default toward our acquired values, this is what others will notice about us; this is what attracts or repels them. We may even get into a relationship because we like each other's acquired values, without even knowing what our partner's core values are.

For example, Selena used to highlight her acquired values when attracting a person of interest but then turned to her core values once she felt comfortable in the relationship. You can guess . . . every single one of her relationships bitterly failed at this phase. Let me explain.

Selena was always a very successful professional; she started a governmental job and rapidly climbed the ladder of promotion. She also placed a great value on her appearance, regularly exercising, eating healthy, and always dressing in the latest fashion trends. In her encounters with potential dates, Selena tried to seduce them by demonstrating *power, independence, success,* and *appearance* because she had acquired the idea that this is what you need to attract a mate. And she was very successful in doing so.

But once she was comfortable in a relationship and ready to make a deeper commitment, Selena would drift to her core values: *family, education,* and *loyalty.* It was like she had a switch; she transformed completely. The seductive, flirty, well-dressed Selena would give way to a woman primarily focused on getting married and starting a family. Instead of the independent and powerful woman who attracted her partners, she became someone who wanted, more than anything, to be taken care of by her boyfriends. She became needy and clingy. Her partners didn't appreciate this switch—they'd chosen her in the first place for completely different values, which they found attractive. I'd heard Selena say over and over and over again, "Men are all the same. Once they know they can have you, you are not interesting to them anymore, and they start treating you badly."

If we want to find the "right" partners, we have to lead with our core values, showing how our three basic psychological needs are likely to be satisfied. Sure, it's easier to play the part that gets attention from the people we want to attract, but if we are searching for lasting bonding, the masks have to go. By aligning our lives with our core values, we give others permission to do the same. By communicating our core values and needs to our partners, we open the doors for true intimacy. High-quality relationships are those in which partners understand each other's acquired values and willingly *choose* to respect and support each other's core values. By doing so, they support each other's need for autonomy and competence. Research shows that securing this informed and respectful autonomy (not the kind of autonomy that leads to nonconsensual cheating) within relationships means partners are more likely to see problems as challenges rather than annoyances, experience less distress, and are more inclined to work through these challenges.[78]

WHAT'S YOUR PLAN?

If I have to pick one tip for a more harmonious connection, it would be to begin with investing time in understanding each other's needs-values-behavior pattern. Although I worked with many people on their value systems, I've yet to meet a person who fully understood their core and acquired value system, how they got "programmed" and shifted away from their core values, and how acting on those values satisfies their three basic psychological needs. If we don't understand our own patterns, how in the world do we expect to understand our partner's?

So, if you don't have a plan yet, here's what can help.

ACTIONS AREN'T ALWAYS STRONGER THAN WORDS

This is the story of Alex and his wife, Sonia. Although the two of them originate from the same small village in a war-torn country and are of the same age, their families have very different histories.

Ryan, Richard M. and Edward L. Deci. *Self-Determination Theory: Basic Psychological Needs in Motivation, Development, and Wellness.*

Sonia's family decided to wait for the war to be over before rebuilding their lives. They went through some tough times, but, eventually, peace was restored, and the family reunited and enjoyed better days. Or at least so they thought. Over the first war-free summer, they wanted the whole family to spend some time together, so they rented a wonderful house on the French Riviera with a big balcony and a sea view. After dinner, Sonia's mom poured herself another glass of sparkling wine and said: "The struggle is finally over. We're free; we're in peace; we're happy and healthy. Life is good."

A moment later the police called and informed her that a terrible car accident had happened. Her younger brother, driving to join the family, had been in a crash and died. Sonia still recalls with crystal clarity what her mom told her on that day, as a despair Sonia will never forget radiated from her mom's eyes: *Never say that you are happy in life and that everything is good because something is going to happen that instant.* You won't be too surprised to learn that Sonia described her top acquired value as *never be happy with what you have and always strive for more.*

When he was six years old, Alex's family left their native country and relocated to Western Europe, making Norway their permanent home. His parents valued *modesty* and highly appreciated the possibility to escape the war and settle down in the new country. *Be grateful; we are doing fine; we have everything we need* was their motto. Alex grew up valuing *modesty* so strongly that he had trouble accepting a well-deserved promotion because he felt he didn't need it. Modesty was by far his most influential acquired value.

Now Sonia and Alex really love each other, no doubt about that. But imagine them on vacation together. Alex, grateful for the opportunity to live the life his parents could only imagine, and Sonia, programmed on a completely unconscious level to never say that "everything is OK." On vacation, Sonia's commentary went like this: *This room is so small, and we wanted the sea view. They could have added more spices to the fish; it's not that great. There's not enough shade on this beach.* Meanwhile, Alex: *Can't you just once stop being so negative and see all the beauty and privilege we have? Why do you have to complain every single time when we're so lucky and blessed to have all this?* Despite their genuine love, they fought and fought and fought.

This is exactly what happens when we talk on the level of actions, not values. Although Alex knew that Sonia's uncle died in a car accident, I don't think he could have guessed how the entire situation played out for Sonia in her childhood and how she acquired the value *strive for better*. Before the values training, Alex was clueless that this value was linked to Sonia's traumatic experience. When we completed several coaching sessions, and the entire story on their values-behaviors pattern surfaced, both instantly softened. Alex immediately forgave Sonia about complaining, even regretting his criticism. And you could see Sonia's determination to avoid complaining as much as possible. Neither gave up on their acquired values in that instant—that needs more work—but they found a way to understand and embrace each other's acquired values once they knew the whole story. They managed to find a compromise that made them both feel good.

Take a short moment to think about your relationship. Do you really know your partner's stories? Chronically imposed acquired values? Small social traumas?

We judge our partner's behavior and actions, but we so often fail to see in which values their behavior is rooted. If (*if!*) we are paying attention, we can often spot where our partners have picked up some of their bothersome behaviors (wow, my father-in-law really likes to believe that dominance is a virtue . . . so *that's* where he gets it). But if our partner's behavior is due to a small social trauma, it is likely that such behavior will never make sense to us. We will repeatedly blame our partners for doing something wrong. Our communication will always take place on the surface. If we think of two people as two apple trees from Chapter 3, judging people based on their acquired values would be like one apple blaming another apple from a different tree for being too small, without considering what kind of soil or climate affected its growth.

I've seen a number of couples improve their relationship once they understand and embrace both of their partner's sets of values. Together, they start the journey of consciously managing acquired values while bringing more core values into their lives.

ONE PERSON'S GARBAGE IS ANOTHER'S ART—OR, CHALLENGE YOUR DEFINITIONS

Spoken language, as we know it, can sometimes be more of a hurdle than a help in communication. When I say the word *wardrobe*, you think of a piece of furniture designed for storing your clothes and other possessions. Talking about wardrobes and other concrete objects is not difficult. But if I say the word *kindness*, an intangible concept, communication can be challenging. Each of us probably has a unique idea of what kindness means. The same applies to virtually any value. For example, coworkers might have different expectations around the value of *fairness*. Spouses might differ sharply over what *sharing* means. Or they may both hold *closeness* or *loyalty* as a core value, yet the words may mean something different to each.

Yeah, so what, Senka?

Having different definitions of values doesn't sound like a bad thing, right? Isn't it a part of our uniqueness? Yes and yes. Different definitions of values is not a *bad* thing, and it *does* form part of what makes each of us, us. But when it comes to intimate relationships, we can run into trouble when we don't define our terms and share them with each other. Remember Diego and Alicia from Chapter 7? They ran into some relationship trouble because they understand *honesty* and *kindness* differently.

One day, Alicia came home with what she thought was a beautiful antique desk for her new office. When she asked Diego what he thought, he said, "I think it's ugly. It lacks workmanship and taste. It looks like someone's garbage." Alicia turned away, trying to hide the tears in her eyes. *He knows how much I love wood antiques*, she thought to herself. *Why would he say something so aggressive, so unkind?* Hurt, Alicia fired back with a mean comment about Diego's cherished poster collection. Diego, unsure why Alicia had just attacked him out of nowhere, escalated the argument even more . . . you can imagine how it went from there. Not good.

The couple shared this story with me during coaching. I helped them get to the bottom of the conflict by identifying and comparing what core and acquired values were at stake. For Diego, *kindness* and *honesty* are inseparable—you tell someone the truth, even when it might hurt their feelings, because you care for them, and you want to spare them from what you think are the negative consequences of their choices. Diego thought Alicia should know that the desk looked, in his opinion, crappy, and he didn't want her new colleagues to judge her for having a second-hand desk. He thought that's kind.

For Alicia, however, Diego's version of *honesty* felt more like *aggression*. She felt Diego was being unkind. Alicia believes that *honesty* should be balanced with "real" *kindness*. In her case, this means you might not tell someone exactly how things are if you think the brutal truth might hurt them. She would've responded better if Diego had side-stepped his real opinion to offer a neutral response, such as, "I'm glad that you bought something you like" or "I'm sure you will enjoy it, babe."

When Diego heard this, he was annoyed.

"That's not *kindness*. That's *politeness*. That's what I'd say to anyone off the street! Well, not the 'babe' part."

Diego felt that Alicia's version of *kindness* is something reserved for strangers or people you aren't close to. For him, part of loving someone means you can skip the niceties. For Alicia, being *polite* is a way to show *kindness* and, to her, being *kind* is more important than being *honest*, especially with those you love. So, a situation that was, in truth, about two people's different tastes and styles ignited a relationship conflict that caused both people pain.

When we try to impose our ideas about exactly how a value should be expressed in terms of behaviors, we risk a "value clash" that can jeopardize relationships. Although we all start with the same inborn needs, we acquire different values and develop different behavioral patterns to meet those needs. This is why understanding your two value systems *and* your partner's is vital for building a solid relationship and managing conflict. But the key message here is that simply knowing (or naming) a partner's values isn't enough. You need to *understand them the way your partner does*, through their eyes.

THE LONE WARRIOR

One question that I hear all the time, in all different settings is "What do you do when you're the only person aware of the acquired versus core values concept in the conversation?"

It is common for one partner to be heavily invested in self-development, while the other one is not. To be honest, I don't have a bulletproof formula for this one. My most honest answer is that it is very difficult to work it all out on your own. I would always choose to invest some time and energy in bringing my partner onboard. However, I know there are people who are opposed to modern psychology and any kind of self-growth approaches.

Let me share a secret with you: you are not alone. We all have those people among the ones we love the most. When I was developing the concept of core versus acquired values, I needed several "guinea pigs" for a small, pilot, proof-of-concept study. My team offered four intensive ninety-minute coaching sessions for free. In return, our volunteers had to complete three questionnaires and monitor their stress parameters for a period of three months. I asked my sister to participate and she said verbatim, "Please, Senka, please leave me out of this. I'll pay you 20€ not to participate."

What I want to say is that I understand if you can't get your partner involved. Even when I won the McLean Hospital and Harvard Medical School's first place award for research on core versus acquired values and started working with clients from all over the world, my sister never wanted to hear about it. On the other hand, that gave me the extra motivation to work hard on developing strategies for "lone warriors."

Here are some ideas.

The first step is to decide what kind of outcome you'd like to achieve. If you would like to change a behavior that's rooted in someone's acquired values, but you think changing their values is not feasible, the simplified advice would be to understand what those acquired values are and try to talk them in or out of specific behaviors by talking to their values. Talking to *their* values, not *yours, capito*? If this sounds complicated or confusing, let me share an original transcript of a session I had with a client who was in this exact situation with his mom.

Anton: I understand now this idea about values. I find it really amazing that it's so simple, yet I've never thought of it before. Or . . . I've never heard of something like that before. But it makes so much sense to me.

Me: I'm glad it's coming together for you, and I'm happy you are getting something out of this program. Now for the last session, let's see in which area of your life you'd like to apply what you've just learned.

Anton: Sure. First, *family* is really important to me. When I reflected on it at home, my first thought was, *wow, I'd really like to use this concept to improve my conversation with my parents*. Now I understand so much better where they are coming from and why they value so much some things in life. Still, I know I can't just go to them and tell them, "Ooh, those are only your acquired values, let it go."

I also think they have been stuck to those values and beliefs for probably more than sixty years now, and I don't believe I can do anything to change it now . . . It takes time, self-initiative and their wish to learn and change, and I honestly don't believe they have it now . . . So, I really want to use this concept. I only don't get how to use it in a conversation in which you are the *only one* being aware of the concept.

Me: OK, let me tell you one thing I've noticed?

Anton: Sure.

Me: I already see how much you "softened" when you talk about the values of your parents. Last time, I could feel anger, blame, and disappointment. Today, I can hear a really constructive approach—it's inspiring how you let this settle in.

Anton: Thanks. No, it really came all together to me. I was thinking about their generation, parental advice they received, their immigrant background, adapting to a new society, everything. They didn't have it easy. I mean, I was aware of that before. But not so concretely. All the challenges seem much more real to me.

Me: That's a great basis for the next discussion. Can you tell me a recent example of a conversation that went badly between you and your mom or dad?

Anton: Yes, I have one. It happened just this weekend. We had guests at home for lunch. They are just "common" people like us, family people. And my mom was trying so hard to make everything perfect for them; she cooked three different meals, soup, salad, and she even baked her own bread. Now, the bread was not as perfect as it usually is. She bought yeast, or what do I know what, from a new supplier, and the bread didn't rise as she expected.

Now, it looked OK; it was warm and it tasted great. But it made her totally desperate that it was smaller than usual. She immediately started panicking and getting really nervous, and she asked me to go to the bakery—the most expensive one—and to buy a loaf of bread. At that moment I thought, *It's all about her acquired value of public image.* I know it's one of mom's most dominant values. It's always so important to her what will people say, but still, whatever I said didn't help.

Me: What did you say?

Anton: Well, that the bread is really great, that she put so much effort into it, that it tastes perfect, it's such a waste to buy a new one. And it's pouring outside, and I would have to drive . . .

Me: Anton, it seems to me that I can recognize some familiar values in your answer; let's analyze it a bit. For example, "It's such a waste." Where does this come from?

Anton: Um—

Me: What was your definition of saving?

Anton: Let me look. *Never use more than you need.*

Me: What about "It tastes great, although it doesn't look perfect?"

Anton: Modesty? I defined it as: *Always see the positive side, and be happy with what you have.*

Me: What about your rejected value of dominance, which you defined as *opposite of fairness?*

Anton: Yes, when she asked me to drive in the rain and go to exactly that bakery on the opposite side of the city, I really felt she was not being fair and acting as if I didn't have a right to have an opinion. I was so angry at that moment. I drove to the bakery and bought the bread. But I was [explicative for really angry] for the rest of the day.

Me: What bothered you more in this situation, the fact that your mom has this value or that you had to act on her requests?

Anton: This value does bother me, but I don't think I can change it. Plus, now I perfectly understand why she holds on so tightly to this value. But I would feel much better if I would be able to find a way around those actions that don't make any sense to me. But it would have to happen in a normal conversation, so that we don't fight.

Me: OK, I see. Do you know now what was the problem with this conversation?

Anton: No, and that's the problem (laugh).

Me: From whose value system did your arguments come and from whose value system did your mom's arguments come?

Anton: Oh, wow. (ten seconds of silence) All my arguments were only from my own *acquired* values. I haven't even noticed . . .

Me: What was your mom's value in this situation?

Anton: Public image. What other people think of her.

Me: How could you argue from her value system in this situation?

Anton: I could say something like, "Hey Mom, I can drive to the bakery, but what do you think will look better to our guests? Some company-baked bread that has who-knows-what inside or the homemade, still warm bread that you baked yourself, only for them? I think they will find the option two way better, what do you say?"

Me: How do you think your mom would react to this?

Anton: Differently . . . yes.

Me: What can you learn from this?

Anton: Well, many things. First, I could have checked what values of mine were active. I've noticed that I'm angry and upset—I could have immediately recognized a rejected value. Second, arguing from my own value system with someone who has a completely different value system is not the most productive way (laugh). I could have also asked myself, what would be a good outcome of the situation for me, and I could try to talk my mom out of her ideas by talking to her value system. At least I would have a chance to be listened to (laugh).

No, seriously, this was so helpful to look back at the situation with a different set of eyes. I get it better and better . . . But I still think it's a long way ahead of me. I hope one day this will become a more automatic way of thinking than it is now. I'm sure it will—just have to practice. But it feels great to have a better overview and direction.

All Aboard!

But if you would like to "dig deeper," beyond just influencing a loved one's behavior (i.e. help them close their Rhetoric-Reality Gap), then you'll have to take another approach. In my experience, pointing out what the other is doing "wrong," no matter how nicely you say it, is not the way to go. A softer approach, where you'll act from the standpoint of curiosity, is usually a better option.

When you notice your partner acting differently from what you think is best for them, you may want to take an observer's role. Instead of blaming them, you can try learning about them. What remnant of the past makes them act in this way? Whose voice is pressing on them? From your curiosity to learn about their patterns, you may *indirectly* raise their own awareness around their acquired values, beliefs, behaviors, gremlins of the past, and beasty Chihuahuas. Take a look at how my coaching client, Kat, improved her relationship without dragging, threatening, or ultimatum-ing her partner . . .

Kat was tired of her boyfriend's flakiness. He was always late, forget important dates and details, and need to be reminded three times about plans, including family visits. She told me she felt like she was always nagging and complaining—attitudes and behaviors that were not serving her wellbeing. She really wanted to get her guy to join us in our coaching sessions and wanted to share what she'd been learning about her core and acquired values. But, alas, he severely resisted taking even one session.

So, together, Kat and I tried to figure out which of *her* acquired values was rearing its ugly head. We came down to one of her *big* acquired values—*responsibility*. Using what she learned about her own value systems, Kat tried to understand which values were important to her boyfriend by carefully listening to him. Sometimes, she would even write down whole conversations and share them with me. She figured out that one of his top core values was *freedom*. He was passionate every time he spoke about it.

With that knowledge, Kat began to modify her behavior. She stopped yelling every time he acted "irresponsibly" and, over time, the guy noticed her change. One day he asked, "Why aren't you yelling at me?" He'd come to expect it from her. Kat clued him in on how she'd changed her behavior as a result of her values training. He was interested. And, just like that, they were having a helpful conversation about expectations and values. The rest is history.

Does this take time? Yes, a lot of it. Does this take energy? Yes, a lot of it (just ask Kat). Changing an old thinking pattern is quite a process (you can also consider giving your partner this book to do the job for you).

Once you understand your partner's acquired values and related behaviors, you can work on identifying your partner's core values, passions, and intrinsic motivation triggers. Finally, you can start discussing how their acquired values create roadblocks between their current self and their best self. Although your initial impulses may tell you differently, those situations are gifts, even if the conversation doesn't always go as smooth as silk. They are opportunities to truly get to know your partner. Eventually, *To Know You (Is to Love You)*[79], so said Bobby Vinton half a century ago.

Does this process pay off? Yes, getting your partner onboard to jointly work on understanding core and acquired values is one of the best things you can do for your relationship.

If You Love Me, Show It

"Of course I care about my partner's wellbeing!" said Tamara, almost offended, during our initial coaching conversation.

"Great, tell me in which ways your partner satisfies his three basic psychological needs and what do you do on a daily basis to support them?" I asked.

"What?" Tamara looked at me as I'd asked her something in Japanese.

Tamara's reaction is not uncommon. Not only do our upbringing and conventional education often fail to systematically teach us about our needs and healthy ways to meet them, we enter adult relationships with next to zero training on how to support a partner's needs for autonomy, competence, and relatedness. Now that you are well-trained in satisfying your own basic needs, it's time to devote some of that mindful awareness to your loved ones. By paying attention to the basic needs of others, you'll notice when current circumstances are thwarting one of them. And you'll need to make an extra

---

79   Bobby Vinton, "To Know You (Is to Love You)." *Vinton*. Epic Records, 1952.

effort to acknowledge the situation and give them space to work on this need when the time is right.

For example, if you have a newborn at home, it is very likely that a primary caregiver who looks after the baby in her first months will face challenges in meeting their need for autonomy and/or competence. Therefore, it is extremely important to acknowledge the time and energy invested in the relatedness and caring for the baby. You might consider supporting your partner with comments like:

> *You are doing such an important job by caring for our baby and investing yourself into this relationship. I know your own personal plans and goals are on sort of standby. This makes what you do for the baby even more valuable. And I want you to know, I am sure that when you return to working on your other goals—this "break" will bring you more strength, motivation, awareness, and creativity. (Or whatever core values they're temporarily not pursuing, but longing for).*

Or if your partner has a bad period at work for whatever reason, their need for competence will be tested. A failure to recognize and support a partner who is struggling can make a tough situation worse and may have negative consequences for your relationship down the line. But if you find ways to support your partner's competency in a way that is helpful to *your partner*, even a challenging situation can bring you two closer together. You might consider intentionally letting your partner invest more time in an important project, brainstorming together about the challenging situation, encouraging them regularly, offering to assist them with their tasks, or simply asking your partner how best you can help and support them during this time.

I can imagine some of you might be thinking something like, *Yeah, right. And how am I supposed to do that, when I barely manage to juggle my own crap?* And I totally understand your point. Our hectic, high-paced world makes it hard to devote as much time to others as we'd like. Yet, the newest research shows that the most successful relationships are those in which both partners are truly committed. This means they deliberately *choose* to genuinely give to their partner for the greater good of the relationship. Relationships that last happily are motivated by a commitment to growth (e.g. to make a partner happy or promote intimacy in the relationship), not by fear (e.g. to avoid conflict or feeling guilty). And, if you willingly give to your partner, make sure you know you are giving what they value the most.

X MARKS THE SWEET SPOT

By now you've spent some time assessing the various *shoulds* in your own life—their origin and meaning to you and whether or not they represent values that serve you. You're on your way to releasing yourself from negative emotions and limiting beliefs. Yay.

However, I am convinced—I really, truly, honestly believe—that a relationship can't work without consciously or unconsciously understanding and embracing our partner's *shoulds*. Those *shoulds* and *should nots* that flicker through your brains when you experience conflict are your treasure maps. Follow them, slaying the dragons, avoiding booby traps, quicksand, and red herrings, and you just might find gold. Every moment of conflict is a potential time capsule—a buried treasure box—containing the secrets to what makes your loved one the person you love. If you dedicate the time, together, to sifting through each other's values, you'll unearth a wealth of wisdom. Instead of judgments, you'll find stories, unexamined emotions, long-held beliefs, tears, and maybe even laughter. Follow the maps, and you'll find that *X* does indeed mark the spot— that sweet spot of open curiosity more valuable than any pirate's booty (except maybe Johnny Depp's in *Pirates of the Caribbean*).

Chapter 11

Raise Kids Who are Self-confident and Fulfilled

O nce upon a time, a little boy was playing in the park, happily driving his tractor toy on the hilly area, when another boy came and grabbed his tractor. The tractor toy thief pushed the little boy away when he tried to hang onto his toy. As the little boy watched the thief play with his toy, his developing brain was processing what had just happened. He didn't cry or shout out. You could see him assessing the situation, figuring things out.

But before he managed to do or say anything, along came Father saying, "You have to fight back, son! You can't just let him push you around!" The more Father told him what to do, the more confused and frustrated the little boy became. It was then that he started crying. What moments before had been confusing was now scary. Father was angry. *I did something wrong*, the little thought to himself, *something about* me *must be wrong*. Now he really *did* feel bad.

Sound familiar? If you're a parent (or if you've ever spent any time around kids), you'll have seen situations like this. A lot. Because we all have our values, I'm sure you have an opinion about what the little boy *should* have done. Or what the toy thief *should* have done. Or what the other boy's parents *should* have done. And you probably have some opinions about how Father handled the situation. Maybe you're silently saluting Father's timely intervention. Or maybe you're thinking, *What was Father thinking?*

In this situation, Father was faced with a choice: act on his own values (to be strong, you have to fight back) or let his kid find his own way to handle the situation and react only when and if given a sign. Father was certainly afraid that if his boy didn't stand up for himself, he'd fall short of something later in life. He wanted to teach him to be *strong*. But what if the little boy had managed to control his anger and continued playing with something else, wouldn't he also have demonstrated *strength*?

We often assume that a self-confident child must be an extrovert or a child with a dominant personality. Wrong. A self-confident child is any child who feels perfectly fine exactly the way they are—the one who feels awesome and comfortable in their own skin. So, how do we know when we need to step in or when to leave kids alone? What do we do when we're sure we know what's best, even though it goes against our kids' natural inclinations? How do we, as parents, negotiate between what our values tell us about how our kids *should* be/act/look like while also raising well-adjusted, confident, happy kids? You're right; it has something to do with basic needs and values. Theirs, not yours.

Look, parenting is hard. If you're reading this as a parent or a parent-to-be, you'll know that as soon as you have kids, everyone wants to tell you how to raise them best. Even strangers off the street. I want you to know that I value and appreciate that people have different styles of parenting and different methods for handling conflict. In this chapter, I'm only going to talk about the "bigger picture" and offer you a framework for parenting. Within this framework, you'll find room to incorporate your own parenting philosophies for promoting safety, good manners, and an ordered and enjoyable atmosphere at home. Because raising children can be so fraught, whenever you feel insecure or in doubt, professional help should be the option of choice.

THE HOLY GRAIL

Research shows that parents are doing quite well (on average) when it comes to our kids' need for relatedness (we aren't interfering too much in their choices of friends and companions), and a bit worse when it comes to their need for autonomy (we still try to talk them out of doing stuff that we've decided isn't right for them . . . although, we are getting better at saying, "Sure, give it a try.").

When it comes to our children's need for competence, however, we've got some work to do. Most of us are still imposing our values about what it means to be competent onto our children. This manifests itself most often as our tendency to interfere with their career choices. We will interfere for decades until our kids have no idea what they actually want to do. We don't do this because we're bad parents or interfering jerks. Many of us fear that our kids won't succeed, will fall short or fall behind, or fail to find happiness in life, and this fear drives our parenting. We want our kids to have the best, be the best, and be happy. Interestingly, we tend not to channel this fear onto our children's choices of partners or personal hobbies in the same, exaggerated way. Instead, we are convinced that our kids need to find "a good job," and that, somehow, finding a good partner and having money to pursue hobbies will automatically follow. Our thinking tends to go like this: *Get a good job, and you'll have a good life* and not *be a good person* or *be passionate about what you do, and you'll have a good life*.

Although this has been very true for parents who are civics and boomers, even today's younger parents work really, really, really hard to instill in their children the skills *they* believe will be essential for doing well in life, career-wise. When asked about modern parenting in an interview for the *The Atlantic* in 2020[80], author and journalist Anne Helen Petersen bluntly pointed to the core of the problem. Parents perceive, consciously or subconsciously, *everything* their children do, from painting and solving puzzles to learning how to swim or ride a bicycle, as a way to reach the Holy Grail—an entry ticket to the college that will secure stable future.

1 + 1 = Who Knows?

Surely one of the most maddening and mystifying and marvelous parts of parenthood is the sheer impossibility of knowing what our children will be and look like. We speculate about how our genetic combinations might turn out or fantasize about "dream team" kids who exhibit the best parts of us. One client of mine still remembers her mother's disappointment that she didn't turn out the way her mom had hoped, with "my blue eyes and your father's black hair." Yet our kids are so much more than the sum of their parts. Sure, who our kids are

---

80 Pinsker, Joe. "How Boomer Parenting Fueled Millennial Burnout." *The Atlantic*, 2020.

and who they will become is partly due to their combination of genes, but it's also, as we've discussed in previous chapters, due to the environment in which they grow up. There's not much we can do about our child's genetic inheritances, but we *can* actively work to create a loving, supportive environment that fosters their intrinsic motivations and pursuit of core values.

As children grow up, it's vital they find a way to unleash their intrinsic motivation. And when it comes to intrinsic motivation, kids function pretty much the same as adults—acting on their core values releases the powerful force of self-determination. Missing out on the energy our kids can gain from engaging in the activities that light up their intrinsic motivation is a huge waste. So, what can we do to make sure our kids are profoundly invested in their core values?

ACTIVELY OBSERVE

The key to noticing and understanding your kids' core values is learning to actively observe. To "actively" observe your child, you will have to quiet the sound of your little Chihuahua, saying things like, *I had an experience just like that* or *this is what Uncle Dan used to do when he was young,* or *she should fight back, not just walk away.* Left unchecked, these voices will urge you to get involved and—instead of learning about your child—your attention will be on projecting your own fears, beliefs, stories, judgments, emotions, and itches.

You will have to take an observer role and establish a laser-like focus on your child's intuitive preferences and responses to external inputs. This means being intentional with noticing your kid's energy and how that energy is changing and leads to array of behaviors; being able to quickly pick out sadness, excitement, and shifts in attitude. Only in this "intentional" state can you truly learn about their core values and intrinsic motivation.

And no, I don't think you have to stay in this hyper-aware state 24/7. There will certainly be moments when your parental instincts will make you take action instead of just observing (the choleric mom writing this assures you that this is perfectly fine). Don't worry; you will get plenty of chances to observe your kids. Your child will constantly revisit their significant behaviors. It is what they will *choose* to do over and over and over again, especially if you don't apply any pressure to them. You will have years to figure out their patterns and interests.

Don't get discouraged if you don't seem to have figured it out, even after observing for a while. If what you notice looks random at the beginning, just keep noticing. When your kids are able to make conversation, ask as many questions as possible about their experiences.

- What made them do this or that?
- What was the most difficult choice of the day?
- What felt good about it?
- What do they think would be the most fun way to spend the afternoon?

When they are a little older, give them an option to create a weekend activity plan. Be creative. Enjoy the learning process!

FACILITATE SPONTANEOUS ACTIVITY[81]

As parents, contrary to what many of us assume, our primary task is *not* to fill in the "clean slate" of our children's brains with our recipes for happiness and success. Our job as parents is to let our children try out things, have new experiences, and see for themselves what they enjoy and what they don't find all that exciting. Our job is to give them the *fair* opportunity to explore the world. Our job is to observe and then facilitate. The more restrictions we place on our kids, the more we cut off ways for their intrinsic personality or "psychological DNA" to express itself.

However, it's still important that these opportunities exist within a list of rules that will ensure they are safe enough. Our kids still need and benefit from boundaries. Putting fingers in the electric socket is not a life experience we want our kids to have (I know because I tried it). As a parent, you will have your own ethical and moral compass that guides your family's rules and safety.

There is one little catch here though: the line between *facilitating* and *being a cheerleader* is very fine. By doing the later, you may replace intrinsic motivation

---

81 To deepen your knowledge on (neuro)science-based parenting, I highly recommend Gregory Careman's (Brain Academy) online class, "Neuroscience for Parents: How to Raise Amazing Kids" offered on the Udemy platform.
URL: https://www.udemy.com/course/neuroscience-and-parenting/
I found inspiration for the metaphor "clean slate," safe parenting framework, and cheering along the way in Gregory's course.

with an extrinsic one, having your child do things for the attention he or she gets out of it. *Facilitation* of the child's spontaneous activity, which means non-intrusiveness and an absence of inflated approval at the same time, is on the other hand, the core of a nurturing environment.

I was recently at a birthday party for a friend of my son's, and I had the opportunity to observe two little boys playing a simple game while their moms sat nearby. I was fascinated—not by the boys—but by the stark differences between the two mothers' behaviors. One mother was right in there with her child, meticulously counting how many points her son had won and telling him what to do to get more points and win the game. The other mother had a more hands-off approach. She watched her son but didn't offer advice or interfere with his play. As it turns out, her child began to win more points, or in this game, sparkly, plastic diamonds. As her son gathered more diamonds, he began to lose interest in the overall game. He had more fun playing with the plastic gems, sorting them by colors. He even turned to his opponent at one point and said, "Look, I have two blue ones, do you want one?" His body language was laid-back, relaxed. Meanwhile, the other boy's mother pushed for the boys to continue playing, encouraging her son to make a comeback. Her son looked anxious and tense. It was clear from his body language that he felt the pressure from his mom. He certainly wasn't enjoying the game more as a result of his mother's coaching. Later, these same boys participated in a foot race outdoors. The boy who'd rather play with diamonds than win them suddenly turned extra-engaged and competitive.

What I hope this illustrates is the value of paying attention to where our children's interests and behaviors take them naturally and to avoid framing or judging those interests and behaviors with our own values. The boy who lost interest in winning diamonds wasn't "weak" or "unfocused," he simply wasn't motivated by the game. Instead, he expressed his intrinsic motivation for achievement and winning during the foot race. And he did this without interference from his parents.

Once you have identified which values trigger your kids' primary motivation, their endless source of energy, or joy, you have to be aware of the following: If you try to influence or point them in another direction, you are taking their biggest power source away from them.

STAY OUT OF THE WAY

As a mother of two, I witness daily how parents try to interfere with the natural choices of their children. What they do may look innocent, and I'm sure they want to teach their children the most helpful things in life, but if it is not in alignment with the child's nature, it may be harmful.

When we try to manage our kid's choices, interests, or the way they react to certain situations (which is due to their character traits and their "psychological DNA"), we send out the message that there is something wrong with their inherent interests or their character. And that is the definition of how to mess up self-confidence. Children's self-confidence is shaped between the ages of two and ten, which makes these years the most important when it comes to supporting their natural interests and character.

At the time when our self-confidence is developing, the part of the brain responsible for more complex thinking processes is not fully operational, and we don't have the brainpower to put things in context. During these developmental years, our children simply don't yet have the maturity to think things like, *My dad surely thinks I'm great, and he actually wants to support my true nature. As the result of his own failures and fears, he's just trying to encourage me so that I can avoid some obstacles he had faced.* Nope. Inside our kids' brains, it's more like, *My dad says I shouldn't act like this. When I act like this I'm not good enough.*

We may inadvertently harm our child's self-confidence when we try to "correct" their behaviors. Particularly when they're young, children's feelings about themselves are heavily influenced by how others feel about and treat them, especially their parents or guardians. If they grow up hearing that whatever they do isn't good enough (even when we don't really mean it), how are they supposed to grow into an adult with a positive self-image? The shame accumulated from perpetually "failing" feels painful, and kids will do anything to avoid this feeling, even going against their own natural instincts and passions.

"Your words today will become your children's inner voice tomorrow."
—Peggy O'Mara

It may take some time for the effects of going against their true nature to show up. Often, the consequences of our criticism have a delayed and cumulative effect. When I think about the "time-released" effect our words can have on our kids, I always think about my school friend, Steve.

As a kid, Steve was naturally extroverted. He was the class clown and loved telling stories and jokes during every family or school gathering. And goodness, he had the most refined sense of humor I've ever encountered in my life. One day, while telling a story in front of his school friends (who listened in awe and laughed until they were out of breath), an uncle interrupted saying, "You should put as much effort into your homework as you do into your dumb stories." He was half-teasing, but Steve wasn't old enough to understand the nuances of adult behavior. And his own parents didn't help, "This is what I'm telling him every day," his mother said. See how poor Steve encountered chronical value acquiring *and* the small social trauma simultaneously? While Steve didn't change his extroverted ways right away, the result of being humiliated by his uncle in front of his friends and perpetually by his parents inside their four walls showed up later in life. As an adult, the once outgoing and boisterous jokester who could have been a star with his unique talents (as an actor, comedian, or kindergarten teacher, for example), Steve opted for a "regular," more secure and stable office job—which he got only after years of dreading school and swapping universities. Steve's extraordinary talents went to waste and, at age forty-five, he's still struggling. He's been treated for his alcohol addiction three or four times. The last time I met Steve's mom, she told me: "I wish my Steve could have done things differently—finished law school like his friend Bruce or civil engineering like Stela—but he just couldn't. He was always so unmotivated." My heart was breaking for Steve, and I wanted to yell, "Well, yes, you are right; he just couldn't. And no, you are not right—he was incredibly motivated, until a boatload of acquired values blocked his way."

We can't shield our children from every acquired value out there, nor should we blame or judge ourselves when we slip up. The message in Steve's story is that our kids are listening and what we say to them matters, more than we know. Steve's mom thought he didn't care about what she was telling him. I know Steve cared so much that he was willing to give up his authenticity to win her approval. Because this is too high price to pay, just stay out of the way. (I'm getting poetic.)

Avoid Small Social Traumas

As we discussed in Chapter 5 and have seen in many examples, small social traumas are breeding grounds for value formation. How can we prevent small social traumas from turning into ugly monsters and angry Chihuahuas? Establishing rules about a few important things can help.

- Teach your kids to give their ideas more than one chance. It's important for kids to get the message that they won't always win, that sometimes they will fail or not get what they want. But that doesn't mean their ideas are worthless. It doesn't mean *they* are worthless. It may help you to tell your kids that Walt Disney's ideas for Mickey Mouse were rejected 100 times before he found a producer willing to give his cartoon a chance.
- Teach your children how to flag important ideas and emotions. It's normal for us to tune out our kids from time to time. For one thing, they talk *a lot* and *all of the time,* once they start. For another, much of what they say just isn't interesting to us, and we're busy trying to do a thousand other things. We aren't interested in what Maya B. (not Maya F.) did at school or why unicorns are more powerful than dinosaurs. Due to the sheer volume of stuff our kids say when they're younger, it's important for them to have a way to get our attention when it matters. For example, I am teaching my kids to say, "Mom, I want to share something really important with you" when they have something important to tell me.
- Be really careful with scary topics, such as death, failure, and public humiliation. Remember how much Sonia's mother's reaction to her uncle's death affected her? It had consequences into her adult life. The same goes for the "teasing" friend Steve received from his family. Just be mindful that some topics need specific attention and care.

DON'T ASSUME (DON'T MAKE AN A$$ OUT OF U AND ME)

When my friend Ly was a girl, she loved to read. Left alone, she could read for hours and hours, finishing chapter books in one day. This behavior was obvious to her parents, and they nourished her love of reading with library cards and plenty of books. How nice, right? Certainly Ly, now grownup, appreciated her parents' support as she pursued a core value. But in focusing solely on the most obvious of Ly's natural interests, they didn't pay attention to how much she *also* liked to be outdoors and do active things. She loved to swim and was fascinated with ice-skating. But, outside of mandatory swim lessons and a few rare trips to the ice rink, Ly's parents didn't offer her opportunities to explore her active, physical self. Overlooking the different and various things that sparked Ly's intrinsic motivation was their first misstep.

Secondly, Ly's mom, while she appreciated her daughter's love of words, assumed that kids who read books must not be good at sports. In her mind, kids were either "nerds" or "jocks," and if you were one, you couldn't *also* be the other. During her childhood, Ly's mom repeatedly told her, "sports and athletics just aren't your forte, honey." Over time, Ly stopped begging for ice-skating lessons. She didn't join any clubs or teams that involved physical activity, and she told herself that she "just wasn't good" at sports. It wasn't until she was in her twenties that Ly realized she *was* a sporty and athletic type. *And* a book-reader and nerd. She started doing yoga and trained to run a half marathon. Although she now regularly incorporates outside activity in her mostly happy life, sometimes Ly wonders what she missed out on (high school sports teams, new friendships, and different experiences) as a result of her parents' lack of attention and assumptions.

What's the lesson here? Some of our kid's core values are easy to spot and easy to facilitate. But if we stop at the obvious and aren't actively observing our kids, we may miss out on showing our kids all of what life has to offer. We may, consciously or unconsciously, channel them into narrow understandings of their own selves and abilities. We may give them less of the world instead of more. We may overlook opportunities to nurture the diverse ways our children's delightful curiosity engages the world around them.

Don't Fret—It's Not Too Late

Now, I have to say, it's not the end of the world if, when you read this, your children are all grown, and you've already done the job of projecting and imposing your own values onto your kids. Your kids might have become really good in something they don't like the most. They may end up successful and socially recognized, living a very good life and enjoying their jobs. But, in the end, to live a life true to them and be fully authentic, they *will* come back to the things that trigger their intrinsic motivation later in life.

My own adult life is a perfect example. As a child and teenager, I did well in STEM (science, technology, engineering, and math) subjects. As a result, my parents channeled me toward the hard sciences. And I've been a successful biochemist, with fancy awards and postdocs and now a team of students and employees.

Meanwhile . . . I have always been an empathetic person. Even as a child, I would laugh and cry alongside others and try to relate to people on an emotional level. My parents weren't oblivious to my intrinsic motivation; they just never considered that it could lead to a career. But this isn't a story about regret and missed opportunities. Neither is it a story about guilty parents. When we (or our children) are passionate about something, we will return to it. We cannot totally leave our core values behind. I found exciting ways to incorporate motivating others into my day job—I teach PhD students from three different universities in Graz how to extract and leverage their core values in ever-challenging academic environment. In those classrooms, I'm fully pursuing my core values of *empathy* and *caring*. Being immersed in biochemistry and psychology turned out to be an incredible advantage at the end of the day. It keeps my awareness that our bodies and its molecular processes are inseparable from our thoughts and feelings (a lesson that every natural scientist must keep in mind).

So, don't fret. You haven't ruined anything. You may have made your kids take a detour, but this detour may be full of valuable experiences and may actually lead them back to their most authentic selves in even better, unexpected, exciting, and wildly rich ways.

BEYOND MARRIAGE AND KIDDOS

These strategies for improving relationships I've shared with you in the last two chapters are universal; they go beyond marriage or parent-child relationships. You may use these strategies to improve friendships, relationships among siblings or any other significant connection you care about. Discussing values, not only actions and behaviors, is *always* a good idea. When we understand each other's acquired values and embrace each other's core values, we create a rock-solid foundation that can withstand the many challenges that will inevitably show up in long-lasting relationships.

Chapter 12

Love Your Work

"**H**ey Zac, how are you; how was your weekend?" I casually asked my colleague, as I dropped my bag and reached for my lab coat. Instead of an expected, "Good, how was yours?" my colleague surprised me that particular Monday morning with words that keep coming back to me (or I keep coming back to them?) many years after they filled our 130-square-foot office for the first time.

"I was thinking a lot," Zac said. "In the last five years since we've been working together, I've seen my PhD student Malik more than I've seen my children. Also, for every hundred hours at work, I probably scored one hour doing what I'm really passionate about. And yet, I consider myself to be the lucky one in terms of career. Many of my friends in other career paths ("age-matched controls") feel much worse. So, I again caught myself wondering if this is how life should be or should I radically change something?"

Zac's unexpected disclosure pretty much summarizes how a great number of people, at least in the Western world, feel about their jobs. The majority of US workers across nineteen industries said they are unhappy with their jobs, according to a survey conducted by Mental Health America and the Faas Foundation. On top of that, a whopping 71 percent of employees are looking for new jobs or a career change.[82] Even classically "successful" high performers, as my colleague Zac, who worked hard to follow "the success formula" and achieved substantial personal and professional goals, still feel stuck. And when people feel stuck, their wellbeing is stuck too, spilling the "stuck-ness" to other areas of life.

RUNNING ON EMPTY

We touched on the important role our work has in a well-balanced, meaningful life when we were discussing juggling our three basic psychological needs in the Chapter 1. Although this is something we *know*, we surely let it slip our consciousness too often. So, let's remind ourselves of the trap we can run into when we pursue an unfulfilling career for extended period of time. The absolutely worst *long-term* mistake we make is choosing a job that satisfies our desire for money or reputation but fails to meet any of our three psychological needs.

We all have twenty-four hours a day to do with them what we think is best for us. And we all have three basic psychological needs to satisfy. After removing time spent on sleeping and necessary chores and taking into account that working, commuting to work, thinking about work, and worrying about work take up ten or twelve hours a day, we are left with only a few hours a day to take care of our relationships, our autonomy, and our competence. And this, my friends, no matter how hard we push ourselves, simply can't work. No matter how hard we try, we're poised to struggle due to conflicting schedules and the sheer impossibility of adding more hours to a day. We end up trying to cram our longing for adventure, family time, and working on our own passions or business projects into the same few hours. We feel guilty when we neglect our loved ones to work on our dream projects, and we feel guilty when we stop pursuing those dream projects to do something else. We can end up resenting our loved ones for taking us away from our passions and hobbies, and our loved ones can end up resenting our passions and hobbies for taking up the time we could be spending

---

82   Michele Hellebuyck, Theresa Nguyen, Madeline Halphern, Danielle Fritze, Jessica Kennedy. "Mind the Workplace: MHA Workplace Health Survey 2017." *Mental Health America and The Faas Foundation*, 2017, accessed February 22, 2021, https://www. mentalhealthamerica.net/sites/default/files/Mind%20the%20Workplace%20-%20 MHA%20Workplace%20Health%20Survey%202017%20FINAL.PDF.

with them. Inevitably, one area of our life will always come short. Full disclosure: it's not only from my clients that I've learned these lessons.

So, unless your work is already filling your "wellbeing tank," regardless of where you are in terms of your career and life situation, your *long-term* top priority is to engage in a kind of work that will satisfy your needs for *autonomy* and *competence*.

Did you notice that I left *connection* out of that previous sentence? Good. You're officially a basic needs expert! I didn't include it because most of us form our most meaningful relationships outside of work, and we need time away from the office to nurture those relationships. But even if you work alongside your bestie or spouse, you'll need (and want) to spend time together doing something other than work.

I am emphasizing the long-term because we all have shorter periods of time when doing something other than our dream job is necessary. I was twenty-one years old when my dad died of a stroke. He was the primary breadwinner, and his death sent our family into an economic crisis. We all had to help out to make ends meet. I was only halfway through my studies and had no choice but to take jobs where I wouldn't need many qualifications. So I spent eight hours a day in a warehouse, sticking product information stickers on boxes of goods for a company that produced kitchenware. If I'd heard a word about a fulfilling career or "dream job" at that time, I'd probably have slapped the source in the face.

ONE SMALL STEP FOR YOUR CAREER, ONE GIANT LEAP FOR WELLBEING

Once you're in a situation where you can start moving in the direction of that dream job, do it. No matter how tiny the steps, take them. Studies have shown that performing well on a task we think we *should* do (a task rooted in our acquired values) rather than *feel driven* to do (a task rooted in our core values), does not reliably enhance perceived competence or lead to better wellbeing and vitality.[83] That means even if you are best in what you do, if your competent activity results from your "should," it will lack the important positive effects that

---

83   Nix, Glen A., Ryan, Richard M., Manly, John B. and Edward L. Deci. "Revitalization Through Self-Regulation: The Effects of Autonomous and Controlled Motivation on Happiness and Vitality." *Journal of Experimental Social Psychology*, 1999.

you gain when you feel competent at an activity linked to your core values. (If you need a reminder of what that looks like, go back to Chapter 9 and remind yourself what you would do in your perfect month, *Minister of . . .*)

Although it's crucial for our wellbeing, experiencing autonomy and competence through our work has multiple positive effects beyond a happier life for us. The SDT research documents that we more robustly express our curiosity, creativity, productivity, and compassion in contexts in which our basic needs are supported. So, if you're not currently employed in a way that hits those basic needs, you're not maximizing on your full potential. Not only will you not thrive in company or institution, you won't be the best asset to your company either, which will further influence the negative loop.

You may feel too overwhelmed to even think of a career change right now. Maybe you have an overly controlling boss or only-profit-matters company politics or don't have the financial security to pursue a stage-acting career. Whatever your particular situation, maybe my advice sounds like it's coming from another galaxy . . . still, *worry you should not, with you the force is.* Even if you only take small but continuous steps over whatever period of time you'll need, you will eventually be able to balance the satisfaction of your needs throughout your schedule. This will allow you to be fully present exactly where you are in the moment, be it at work or the beach or in the garage with your model train, without secretly longing for other activities.

To Stay, or Not to Stay, That is the Question?

When we satisfy our need for autonomy and our need for competence by engaging with our core rather than acquired values throughout our working hours, we set ourselves up for deep satisfaction at work. But what happens most often is that our core values, our main ingredients of satisfaction, do not match the values of the organization or company we work for. This happens because we typically have less choice about where we work, and with whom, than we do in other areas of our life. For example, we can choose who we worship with, who we go biking with, who to have romantic relationships with, and usually (or hopefully) our choices reflect our core values. The communities that we *choose* to belong to likely have a lot in common with us when it comes to core values. The same is not always true about the workplace.

Several decades ago, Dr. Norman Feather, Emeritus Professor of psychology at the Flinders University in Australia, recognized that when the individual and organizational values are not a match, the individual—you—are more likely to change and assimilate into your working environment's values and not the other way around. The organization you work for is going to stay the same.[84] Why? Because we are evaluated based on the values of the organization and how well we are advancing those values in our particular jobs. When we find ourselves in such situations, there are two likely outcomes and one less likely:

- We acquire new values to fit the work environment and begin to evaluate ourselves according to the company standards.
- We leave the work environment to find a better fit for our own values.
- We change the culture of the organization (less likely . . . a downer again, I know). If you start a new job as the CEO or president, then, yes, you can make some valuable and meaningful structural changes to an organization's values, but for the rest of us, the burden of change will fall on *us*.

In the long run, a mismatch between ourselves and our work environment is unstable. Sadly, if we leave a job without an awareness of what was behind that mismatch—our core values—we end up finding a new job with a similar misalignment, repeating the same toxic cycle.

If you find yourself mismatched with your work environment, try taking a proactive approach. Evaluate your job and all possible possibilities linked to it in a new light using your newly developed awareness about core versus acquired values. As a result, you'll come to one of the two following conclusions: Either you'll be able to reframe your job responsibilities to align with what you value most and decide to stay, or you'll recognize your current job is a perpetual misfit and use this new clarity to see it as a stepping stone to a more promising career.

---

84   Feather, Norman. "Values in Education and Society." *The Free Press,* 1975.

Bring Your Core Values to Work (Every) Day

Let's talk about the first outcome—choosing to stick it out and make the changes necessary to align your job with your core values. By now, I could probably fill a short book by all the ways I reframed my job to make it better aligned with my values. Reframing my job responsibilities greatly helped me when struggling with my acquired value of *success*, even before I became consciously aware of this process. When reflecting on the addictive nature of my relation to *success*, I noticed another pattern of mine related to winning: every time I was up for something that had the potential to become "more" and lead to a bigger *success*, I worked to include others in my "big quest." I now understand that I was trying to align whatever the situation was with my core value of *motivation* by taking others on board. For most of the projects, I could've done them alone. But I always searched for someone who I felt was in need of a motivation boost to join me. I strongly believe this helped me avoid burn out in my race for winning and made the exhausting race bearable or even enjoyable for most of the time. It was my deep joy in seeing others motivated toward progress, not my academic success *per se*, that kept me going.

Here's another example. I knew I loved science since I was in elementary school. Still, the beginning of my work as a scientist felt so frustrating. After detailed reflection on what wasn't working, I came to the conclusion that my need for autonomy was largely threatened in my early scientific career. My immediate supervisor always wanted a clear hypothesis and a very detailed, structured proposal of my research. She wanted me to come up with a "bulletproof" plan.

For me, on the other hand, one of the most important aspects of feeling autonomous is being a natural observer and following my intuition and "gut feeling." I always enjoyed looking at cells under the microscope and being open to understanding what they might be trying to tell me. Strictly sticking to one protocol and expecting a certain experimental outcome was a very unsatisfying experience for me. When I finally became aware of this, I simply wrote a detailed plan for my supervisor while, in practice, I let myself enjoy the magic of possibilities under the microscope—beyond the expected results of the protocol. My supervisor didn't need to know my little "secret". And I felt in love with my job again.

I currently use this approach on a more conscious level, and I actively seek opportunities and synergies between my responsibilities and my core values. Although one could argue that signaling pathways underlying heart failure doesn't have anything to do with our awareness of need-values-behavior connections, I have noticed an institutional and disciplinary drive toward innovative coaching solutions in health sciences, both as research tools and strategies to improving ever challenging, competitive academic environment. On the other hand, I also noticed a demand for a more scientific approach in coaching. In an era where multidisciplinary, multi-perspective overlap is more celebrated, I feel like I'm helping bridge these two worlds. I realize it may take years of long-term thinking and creative strategies to forge new research paths, and it might be necessary to pursue both in tandem. Still, just knowing I am nearing my ultimate goal, even if it feels like baby steps sometimes—bringing my core values into the very center of my work—makes this a low frustration process led by my most powerful resource, my intrinsic motivation.

By understanding our core values, we can *decide* to bring more of what we most love into our work. And just knowing that we're doing this will work miracles for us.

CHANGING TRAINS

Molly earned her Bachelor of Fine Arts in Visual Art and then went on to get a Master's degree in Art Education. Passionate about art and working with others, she set out on a career as an art teacher. Fast-forward ten years. After a series of jobs in public and private schools, where she watched arts programs disappear one after another, Molly was depressed by how little care was placed on art and expressing oneself in creative ways in the conventional educational system. The budget-strapped schools she worked for had cut their arts programs down to the bare minimum, leaving Molly without the resources to implement her visions for art education and feeling like she wasn't making any difference (*impact* is one of Molly's core values). She couldn't pursue her core values of *vision/imagination* and *adventure/excitement*. She began to resent her work with students because it was seen as needless by the school leadership and was repeatedly the first place to cut the budget in tough times. Molly no longer had the energy or motivation to make her own art. Her health began to suffer.

Finally, Molly decided enough was enough. After years of trying to make it work, trying different kinds of institutions, Molly felt pretty sure the state of art education wasn't going to get miraculously better any time soon. She undertook a serious examination of her core values, life goals, and how she was or was not fulfilling her basic needs. While she enjoyed working in classrooms, the negative effects from her job were higher than the diminishing satisfaction she received from education.

With that knowledge, she researched careers that would allow her to pivot from unappreciated jobs in education to a job where she could use her artistic skills to implement impactful visions and have the time and energy left to travel, go hiking, and more. She sought opportunities that wouldn't require further expensive and time-consuming degrees, and she decided to try the tech field. She found an affordable, online certification program in software programming that took her two months to complete. Once she received her certification, her program connected her with a company that produces software for nurses. They were looking for someone to make instructional videos for their website, which would teach nurses how to use their software.

A month after her phone interview, Molly was on a plane to California. She is still using her graphic design skills and knowing that her work benefits medical health professionals speaks to her core value of *impact*. Molly now thrives, fully immersed in *creativity*, pursuing a career she didn't even think existed less than six months ago.

Although Molly's very true happy ending makes me smile, the message of her experience isn't to quit your job and expect a dream job in three months. What I hope her story illustrates is how Molly made an informed and relatively small adjustment to her life after a thorough evaluation of her core values and intrinsic motivators. After she realized that her top core value of *impact* would likely never be nurtured in her current path, that choice to enroll in a low-stakes programming certificate program led to major improvements to Molly's overall wellbeing. If you know your train is headed in the wrong direction, don't be afraid to get off at the next stop and change trains.

Finding what works for you may require some creativity and possibly even few attempts before you find the right "formula." No matter how frustrating this may feel, in the long run, you will feel significant beneficial effects on your wellbeing.

PLANT YOURSELF WHERE YOU WILL BLOOM[85]

If your current work isn't helping you grow your overall wellbeing, it may be time for my mini Professional Development program. The following practical steps will help you refocus your energy toward a career path that will ultimately align with your core values.

The first step is to identify which of your professional skills and strengths are rooted in your core values. Ask yourself these three questions, and jot down your thoughts in a journal, notebook, Word doc, etc.:

1. **What tasks do I enjoy but others complain about?** Are you the one who gets giddy while crunching the numbers for the books while others dread submitting budgets? Do you enjoy the solo tasks (re-shelving books, filing, doing inventory) that others avoid? Do you enjoy life on the road, traveling frequently while your colleagues try to avoid disrupting their schedules? What was the last task you volunteered for at work?

   For example, Jeff is a scientist and professor at a big university in California. Every three years he volunteers to serve as department chair, an administrative duty that his colleagues try to get out of because it means paperwork, meetings, and less time in the lab. For Jeff, however, being chair also means he gets to spend more time meeting prospective students and implementing policy and curriculum changes that benefit the students, sometimes even going to bat for students against the university's leadership. This aspect of his work engages his core values of *education*, *fairness*, and *community*. And because he loves research, he still makes the time to be in the lab.

---

85 I heard this phrase for the first time from my instructor at the UC Davis coaching program, Jennifer Anderson, and I instantly fell in love with it. It's also the title of her self-published book on "career epiphanies" and turning your gifts into financial rewards.

2. **Where do I get greater returns than the average person?** What makes you stand out at your job? What is the most common positive feedback from your supervisors on your annual reviews/performance evaluations? Is there a particular area or aspect of your job that you are consistently asked to tackle because "no one does it better?"

   A friend of mine used to work alongside the owners and managers of a major international harbor where the rich and famous from all over the world came to dock their yachts. Sadly, most of the higher-ups could only speak the local language. My friend stood out amongst the international captains and wealthy boat owners not only because he could speak the local language, as well as English, French and German, but because of his passion for the diversity of cultures the visitors embodied. Thanks to his genuine interest in different cultures and his communication skills, more people parked their yachts in the harbor, which meant big bucks for his bosses.

3. **What kinds of projects make me lose track of time?** We all know that feeling—when we're so deeply involved in something that time flies by. We skip meals and ignore texts and emails. I can get like that when I am writing—I go deep into my own world and it takes *a lot* to bring me back to reality.

Once you've answered these questions, go back and take a look at your answers. Do you notice any patterns? Repeating words? Where do your answers overlap? Make a note of repetitions and similarities.

Next, using the list of values in the Appendix, see if you can match your professional strengths and preferred tasks with a corresponding value. Does your mania for spreadsheets reflect your value of *order*? Does organizing the annual office parties light up *fun* and *service*? Does talking with patients or students or clients help you express *caring*? Make a list of all of the possible values attached to each of the strengths and activities you identified.

Now, go back to the list of your core values that you identified in Chapter 2. Compare your two lists. Look for overlapping values or connections between the list of your core values and the list of values drawn from your professional strengths. The words don't need to be exactly the same. What you want to look for are general trends and overall similarities. For example, you may have listed *achievement* and *accomplishment* as core values and notice *respect, impact,* or *influence* showing up on your list of professional values. The words aren't the same, but they all speak to someone who values the success that comes from doing something that will raise their profile and earn the admiration of others. Perhaps you mentioned *resources, preservation,* or *contribution* as your professional values and *nature, environment,* or *altruism* as core values. Again, the contexts may differ, but the general meaning of each values cluster is synergistic.

Now that you've identified where your core values meet your professional strengths, it's time to bring more of those values into your work. It sounds simple, but I know that it isn't always straightforward to turn those values into concrete actions.

I wish that I could provide each of you with the perfect solution to your professional woes. But I can't. I can't give you a set of magic strategies that will work for everyone. Each of you has a different job in a different field with different work cultures and structures. Every situation is going to be unique and require your own ingenuity when it comes to problem solving. That being said, I can offer a couple of very adaptable pointers to get you going. If you aren't yet sure how to bring more of what resonates with your core values in your work, you might:

- **Spread the Word**: A colleague next to you might be struggling with exactly the thing that you love to do. Example: I'm quite good at writing academic papers and my colleagues who struggle to make sense and storyline out of their data now call me exclusively for this. Talk with your coworkers and supervisors about what gets you fired up in your job. Ask for opportunities to do more of it—especially if it releases someone who hates doing it from slogging through it. It's a win-win.
- **Move Your . . . Values**: As much as possible, try to move the tasks that engage your core values to the front and center of your work. This will give you more time to keep honing and developing your special

strengths. You'll get more enjoyment from doing stuff that sparks your intrinsic motivation *and* get better and better at it.

- **Buddy Up**: In Chapter 9, we talked about how important engaging the community of like-minded others can be when we want to make a change to our attitude or behavior. This strategy can work really, really well in the workplace. If you can find a colleague who is *also* seeking a similar kind of change, teaming up together to brainstorm, swap ideas, or just listen and provide you with encouragement can make the process more enjoyable.

- **Yes, Coach!** I have witnessed many times how powerful professional coaching can be for people re-evaluating and re-engineering their careers. At a recent conference, a big-name editor of a leading journal shared with us that he had engaged the services of a career/life coach. In front of an audience of hardened, skeptic scientists, he confessed to how much his experience with coaching helped him improve his life and strengthen his career. If you are able, finding a coach is the most surefire way to receive guidance on your own unique career-related questions.

CHALLENGE, ACCEPTED

Well, my courageous reader, you've made it to the end of the informational and instructional part of this book. I've poured everything that I know about values and wellbeing into this book in my best attempt to provide you with all the knowledge and tools necessary to make positive changes in your life. I've drawn from the best and worst of my own experiences, as well as my scientific research, to make the case that our "psychological DNA"—our core values—and the values we pick up along the way—our acquired values—drive our choices. If you've made it this far, it's hopefully because I've been successful in convincing you how important it is to understand your two value systems.

I hope that by now you feel empowered with strategies you can use to re-evaluate and re-shape your life. Your new understanding of the roles that your core and acquired values play in the major aspects of your personality, motivation, relationships with others, and your engagement with your surrounding environments provide you with a powerful advantage when it comes to securing lasting wellbeing.

The rest is up to you. From this moment on, it's up to you to decide what you do with this information. It's easy to nod your head as you read along, agreeing in principle with what I've been saying. And it's pretty easy to answer some reflection questions. But it's even easier to close the book, place it back on the bookshelf (or messy heap of stuff, if you're anything like me when it comes to "creative chaos") and forget about it. Actually taking action, those small but significant steps toward change, requires your active participation and commitment.

My challenge to you is that instead of leaving this book on the coffee table and going about life as usual, make a commitment to making one small change— right now, before you turn the page. What is the one tiny action that you can take today to serve your core values and ignite your intrinsic motivation?

With consistency and commitment, I assure you that what you've learned from these twelve chapters will transform from words on a page into *you*—not a new you, not a "better" you, but the best *you*, living a life grounded in wellbeing and contentment. My big hope is that everyone who reads this book will accept my challenge and choose to act on their new knowledge of themselves. My big hope is that we all decide to be in this together, making the world a better and easier place, a world where we can celebrate together what it means to *be you*.

Conclusion

As I write these words, the world is in the midst of a global pandemic. In the spring of 2020, we watched the numbers of contagions spread in ever-widening circles, red pools on TV or computer screens, and we felt the consequences of stay-at-home mandates as small businesses closed, travel plans evaporated, family lives re-arranged, and many lost their jobs.

The novel coronavirus, COVID-19, is a powerful example of the promises and limitations of our modern society. People across the globe have been coping with unexpected changes and managing multiple expectations and responsibilities simultaneously since the pandemic began. I've seen many working adults drowning in their difficult realities. Many of us spent weeks or months isolated from our family, friends, and neighbors. Conditions such as these challenge all three of our basic psychological needs all at once and our values are being tested on a grand scale.

In time of *en masse* online meetings, I had a chance to reconnect with my friend Marty. We compared our different experiences of the pandemic, me in Austria and he in New Hampshire. Before we closed our Zoom windows, Marty said, "I wonder what the world will look like once I'm holding a copy of your book, printed and published in my hands. Will the crisis help us learn the lessons about our acquired values or will it fuel them with more fear and make them even more fuming?"

My answer to Marty and all of you who may wonder the same thing is—it depends. When we're under pressure (and global crisis puts pressure on all of us), we narrow in on what seems like the safest course of action. And safest action usually means defaulting to our acquired values and the "race for more." The excuses we're giving ourselves may sound all very real—"when the pandemic is over and when things are back to *normal*, I will have more time/energy to think big" —but in a world that seems to put us to the test more and more each day, the collective sense of closure we're waiting for may never come.

The only way to disrupt this trend is awareness. I see awareness as our immune system that can prevent incorporation of acquired values into our "psychological DNA" and protect us from mixing of our core and acquired values. How well we'll do as individuals and society will depend on our willingness to take personal responsibility for understanding and actively managing our two sets of values and their influence on our behavior and wellbeing. When a critical mass of people open to their core values and stop sacrificing their authentic selves to social norms, we'll get a new opportunity. To foster joy, to deeply connect, and to peacefully leave the "race for more." To create the new role models for our children, friends, colleagues, and complete strangers.

The very last thought I want to share with you before you put this book down is to remind you that so many situations are out of our control and will always be. But one thing we'll always have in our hands is a choice about how we approach each day and the expectations we set for ourselves. We'll always have a choice to define what it means to be *me*—the self I was born to be.

Acknowledgments

I always thought coming to this stage of writing was going to be easy. But now, I'm sitting and thinking, *how does one write the acknowledgments for a non-fiction book?* I feel I'd like to thank everyone I ever met for impacting me and helping me have the views, standpoint, awareness, and knowledge of today. So, while I'm thankful to many, here I'm going to acknowledge those without whom the book probably wouldn't exist—at least not for the next decade.

First, I would like to thank my friends, colleagues, and instructors from the University of California, Davis coaching program. Their teachings, stories, vulnerability, and thirst for knowledge were essential for moving forward from vague ideas about values to solid, science-backed strategies for change. Katie Kanowsky was the first to hear about the idea of core versus acquired values. Her sincere enthusiasm about the concept was the fuel I needed to believe that, although I'm a life scientist working in the "molecular" world, my ideas can still be valid in a more practical, social sphere. Without Danielle Collins and our intense and inspiring "Thursday Sessions," I can't imagine having a clear vision for this book, as well as the courage to start writing. Thank you both for being the "godmothers" for *Be You*.

This book literally wouldn't exist without Jennifer Reimer, one of the bravest and most self-aware souls I've met in my adult life. It's hard to define her actual role in the writing process because it fluctuated from friend and editor to a thought partner and coach—and all of those roles together at times. I am so thankful for the chance to know Jennifer and have her—against all odds—living in the same little city in central Europe for a brief moment of our personal histories. *Be You* couldn't have a better "auntie" than Jenn.

Laurie, Heidi, and Steve from *Science2Wellbeing* are the most amazing business partners I could have ever asked for. Laure once said, "We're in this together and for infinity," and there is nothing better in this world that you can hear from a person with whom you intend to pursue the dream vision. With their infectiously enthusiastic spirits, these three manage to inspire me under any circumstances, and they make this cheerful, big, loud family every little baby book needs to have.

A big *thank-you* goes to the Morgan James Publishing team (in order of appearance: Chris and Jim Howard, Taylor Chaffer, Margo Toulouse and David Hancock) for sending me my first-ever Publication Agreement on my birthday (how cool is that?), providing me with excellent, detailed, and up-to-date resources and support, and for matching me with Cortney Donelson for the critical part of the editing process. At every writers' workshop or writing conference I attended, I'd been repeatedly told to get ready because the editing process was going to be brutal and painful. Well, working with Cortney was exactly the opposite—Cortney is an encouraging and knowledgeable editor who works with words with ease, making the whole process smooth and enjoyable and delivered a product I just want to embrace. Finally, to Rachel Lopez who designed a beautiful cover for this book, thank you.

Completing this book would be impossible without my closest friends: Cici, Slatka, Christina, Kaca, and Jelena (x2). I'm honored to embed some of our most important life lessons and most precious memories into these pages, which will be read around the globe! When I think of deep connection, I think of you ladies.

My biggest *thank-yous* go to my family. Thank to my cool Mom, who passionately goes through my ups and downs and never stops learning and improving (even at age seventy!). Thanks Dad, you taught me to dream big and then follow those dreams even when no one believes they are possible (sorry, especially *if* no one believes they are possible). Thanks Ana, my big sister, who maybe didn't want to take part in my coaching endeavors (*see* Chapter 10) but is always there for me in big or small crises. Also, Ana "borrowed" me her BF,

Tomislav, who is a professional book illustrator to work on this project together (when I first saw Tomislav's art many years ago, I said to myself *If I ever write a book, he'll give it a soul with his illustrations*). My parents-in-law gave me the freedom, time, space, and the most amazing view on the Austrian Alps I needed to write this book.

Mkabgvhj nh sfdgf mdithd hg iksjhu are the words for my Michi, simply because there are no real words to describe what he means to me. He's a superhuman dad and the lighthouse of our family.

> **lighthouse** /ˈlaɪtˌhaʊs/ *noun* [C]: A lighthouse is designed to emit powerful flashing light that warns ships of dangerous coastlines, hazardous shoals, reefs, rocks, and shows them the safe entries to harbors.

About the Author

For as long as she can remember, Dr. Senka Holzer has been fascinated by the biochemical connection between our minds and bodies. What began as a youthful curiosity grew into a life-long drive to understand how this connection works. Intuition and scientific interest finally led her to her specialty—heart physiology.

After completing studies in biochemistry at the University of Novi Sad, Serbia, she moved to Graz, Austria, to attend a PhD program in Molecular Medicine from the Medical University of Graz. Soon after graduation, Senka was awarded the Austrian Science Fund's most prestigious postdoctoral fellowship for young female scientists, which led her to the University of California, Davis. While living in California, she entered the world of coaching by completing *Professional Coaching for Life and Work* at UC Davis and *The Science of Happiness* at UC Berkeley.

Senka left the coach-training program inspired to understand whether disconnection from our value systems can have detrimental effects on our hearts. She organized a team of coaches, educators, and scientists to conduct an experimental study on life values and how values-based coaching can change levels of wellbeing and stress. In 2015, she received a research award from McLean Hospital's Institute of Coaching and Harvard Medical School.

Currently, Senka is leading the research unit on subcellular ion homeostasis and hypertrophic signaling in cardiac health and disease at the Department of

Cardiology of the Medical University of Graz and enjoys sharing her work on human values with her students, friends, coaches from all over the world, and total strangers sitting next to her on a plane.

Senka lives in Graz, Austria with her husband and two cutie-pie kids.

Call to Action

Dear Reader—

I hope this book, and its contents have inspired you. Hiring a coach is the best, fastest, and most enjoyable way to implement this newfound knowledge. A coach helps you chart the course of your life by partnering with you to reach your wellbeing goals, using the Values2WellBeing framework and tools.

Contact a Values2WellBeing Coach at: **www.iwantavaluescoach.com**

If you are a coach, and you have connected in a deep way with this work and want to add this powerful work to your professional coaching practice, I'd love to invite you to join Values2Wellbeing Online Coach Certification Program.

Contact us at: **www.beavaluescoach.com**

Values List

Accomplishment	Accountability	Achievement	Action
Adventure	Altruism	Ambition	Appearance
Awareness	Beauty	Bliss	Boldness
Caring	Challenge	Cheerfulness	Collaboration
Commitment	Compassion	Competition	Confidence
Conformity	Consistency	Control	Courage
Creativity	Dedication	Design	Devotedness
Discipline	Dutifulness	Education	Empathy
Endurance	Energy	Enthusiasm	Environment
Equality	Excellence	Expertise	Exploration
Fairness	Faith	Fame	Family
Flexibility	Focus	Fulfillment	Fun
Generosity	Genuineness	Gratitude	Harmony
Helping Others	Honesty	Hospitality	Humility
Humor	Imagination	Impact	Independence
Individuality	Influence	Inner Guidance	Inspiration
Intelligence	Intuition	Joy	Kindness
Knowledge	Legacy	Loyalty	Mastery
Mindfulness	Modesty	Money	Motivation
Nature	Non-Conformity	Non-Judgment	Obedience
Open-Mindedness	Optimism	Order	Organization

Originality
Planning
Power
Progress
Reputation
Self-Expression
Simplicity

Peace
Pleasure
Presence
Prominence
Respect
Self-Reliance
Social Recognition

Perfection
Politeness
Prestige
Purpose
Responsibility
Service
Solidarity

Persistence
Popularity
Productivity
Reliability
Risk-Taking
Sharing
Spirituality

Status
Superiority
Tradition
Vision

Strength
Sustainability
Trust
Wealth

Structure
Teaching
Understanding
Wilderness

Success
Tolerance
Variation
Wisdom

A free ebook edition is available with the purchase of this book.

To claim your free ebook edition:

Visit MorganJamesBOGO.com
Sign your name CLEARLY in the space
Complete the form and submit a photo of
the entire copyright page
You or your friend can download the ebook
to your preferred device

Morgan James
BOGO™

A **FREE** ebook edition is available for you
or a friend with the purchase of this print book.

CLEARLY SIGN YOUR NAME ABOVE

Instructions to claim your free ebook edition:
1. Visit MorganJamesBOGO.com
2. Sign your name CLEARLY in the space above
3. Complete the form and submit a photo
   of this entire page
4. You or your friend can download the ebook
   to your preferred device

Print & Digital Together Forever.

Snap a photo

Free ebook

Read anywhere